My Life in Food

Steven Berkoff

First published in Great Britain by ACDC Publishing 2007

© Steven Berkoff

Steven Berkoff has asserted his right under the Copyright, Designs and Patents Act 1988 to be identified as the author of the book.

A CIP record for this book is available from the British Library.

ISBN 978 0 9556694 0 8

All rights reserved. No part of this publication may be reproduced, stored in a retrieval system, or transmitted, in any form or by any means, electronic, mechanical, photocopying, recording or otherwise, without the prior permission of the publisher, nor be otherwise circulated in any form of binding or cover other than that in which it is published and without a similar condition including this condition being imposed on the subsequent purchaser.

Designed and produced by Andrew Connolly ACDC Publishing
Cover and centre photographs by Steven Berkoff
Back cover photograph by Sheila Burnett

Set in 11/13 point Bembo

Typeset, printed and bound in Great Britain by
York Publishing Services Ltd
64 Hallfield Road
Layerthorpe
York YO31 7ZQ
Telephone 01904 431213
Website www.yps-publishing.co.uk

Acknowledgments
With thanks to Eileen Christopher–Daniels, Brian Daniels, Barry Davis, Karen Dudley, Emma Gordon, Judy Lipsey, Estelle Phillips, Lyn Prendergast and Dorinda Talbot.

STEVEN BERKOFF

Steven Berkoff was born in Stepney in London. After studying drama and mime in London and Paris, he entered a series of repertory companies and in 1968 formed the London Theatre Group. The group's first professional production was *In the Penal Colony*, adapted from Kafka's story. *East*, Steven's first original stage play, was presented at the Edinburgh Festival in 1975. Other original plays include *Messiah: Scenes from a Crucifixion, The Secret Love Life of Ophelia, West, Decadence, Greek, Harry's Christmas, Lunch, Acapulco, Sink the Belgrano!, Massage, Sturm und Drang* and *Brighton Beach Scumbags*.

Among the many adaptations Berkoff has created for the stage, directed and toured are *The Trial* and *Metamorphosis* (Kafka), *Agamemnon* (after Aeschylus), and *The Fall of The House of Usher* (from Poe). He has also directed and toured productions of Shakespeare's *Coriolanus* (also playing the title role), *Richard II* (for the

New York Shakespeare Festival), *Hamlet* and *Macbeth* as well as Oscar Wilde's *Salomé*. He directed and performed in *Massage* in Edinburgh and Los Angeles, *Richard II* at the Ludlow Festival, and has performed *One Man* and *Shakespeare's Villains* at venues all over the world. He has directed his plays and adaptations in many countries including Japan, Germany, Israel, Australia and America.

Films Steven has appeared in include *A Clockwork Orange, Barry Lyndon, The Passenger, McVicar, Outlands, Octopussy, Beverly Hills Cop, Rambo, Revolution, Under the Cherry Moon, Absolute Beginners, The Krays, Fair Game, Another 9½ Weeks, Legionnaire, The Flying Scotsman* and *PU–239*. He directed and co-starred with Joan Collins in the film version of *Decadence*.

He has published a variety of books including the short story collections *Graft: Tales of an Actor* and *Gross Intrusion*, production journals *I am Hamlet, Meditations on Metamorphosis, Coriolanus in Deutschland,* and *A Prisoner in Rio*. He has also published an autobiography *Free Association*, a photographic history *The Theatre of Steven Berkoff*, and travel writing, essay and poetry collections *Shopping in the Santa Monica Mall, America,* and *Overview*. Faber has published Berkoff's collected plays in three volumes, *The Secret Love Life of Ophelia,* and *Requiem for Ground Zero* a tribute to September 11 in verse.

Steven has been involved in a variety of voiceover work, recorded several books on tape, and has exhibited his photographs of London's old East End at several galleries in London. Visit www.stevenberkoff.com

for Clara

CONTENTS

    Preface
1. Joe Lyons Tea Shops
2. Tomato
3. Chicken Soup
4. Hot Dog
5. Rogg's Deli
6. The Bagel
7. Wolfie's
8. Sushi
9. Steak in Cannes
10. Tea at Reids
11. Churrascaria
12. Homage to Grande–Hotel
13. Rascals
14. Breakfast at Itala's
15. Alfredo's
16. Junior's Deli
17. Christmas Dinner
18. Life on the High Seas
19. Simpson's–in–the–Strand

PREFACE

Our lives are shaped by the food we eat, from our first memory of mother's table and even by the dietary laws we observe over what we should or shouldn't put into our mouths.

But for me, as for many, food has had rather more than an emotional impact. I often associate it with happy times, achievements, family and, of course, my mother from whom I first fed. Like most of us I have had cravings for the taste of home when abroad, or in dull–spirited British towns where hotels serve standard, unimaginative junk, and one's mind wanders back to the tasty certainty of mother's wonderful cuisine. Sometimes I have associated food with particular countries and just couldn't wait to get back to that taste, as if the country itself was symbolised by its cuisine and particular dishes, and some restaurants through the world have had a similar effect. I would, I remember,

Preface

rush out of the station at the Gard du Nord and into the nearest café just to smell France – I'd order a coffee and croissant and be perfectly happy.

On one of my first trips back to New York I had to stop the cab taking me to my hotel just to buy a hot dog. It seemed to be a ritual act of imbibing the very nation, of putting America once more inside me even in the humble Nathan's Hot Dog. I was never a grand gourmet fiend so don't look here for any esoteric hints and mouth–watering experiences that chefs have valiantly slaved over. I have a penchant for good tasty food particularly that which has passed through the centuries virtually unchanged. My mother's table was always a feast for me and her dishes had that essential magic ingredient, a poignant taste that clung suggestively to your palate and, of course, your memory zone. I will carry the memories with me all my life. Mum's ancestry was Russian and her mother had passed those dishes down to her. They reflected a time of constant struggle where food was cheap and what comes out of indigence and poverty is naturally invention – a simple earthy beet became the most delirious borscht, the colour of which was exotic and the taste unique. Just a few spuds, provided you had an egg and grated in an onion, would become the most delicious potato pancakes on earth. Without fridges, vegetables had to be preserved in brine and so we had the amazing pickled cucumbers which still adorn every deli table in New York. A scraggy chicken could be metamorphosed into a heavenly chicken soup and all these tastes seemed in

My Life in Food

my young mind to go beyond mere grub for an empty stomach to become something almost religious, and perhaps in some way it was. On Friday night I would visit ma's – the tablecloth would be snow white, two candles would be lit and, as she put the dishes down, it felt that we might have been convening with God himself. So this food became a kind of template for the simple cooking I love. As I explored the world of cuisine I found wondrous other tastes and recall the sheer bliss of my first Chinese in London's Shaftesbury Avenue, of how various and adventurous the food was, and have become a staunch admirer ever since. But not until the eighties did I discover the sensual delights of Japanese cuisine which fulfilled all expectations with its panoply of colours, shapes and subtle flavours.

I grew to appreciate Italian and knew that once in Rome I would be in culinary heaven. But – when eating out – I always need to connect food with some kind of achievement. In Madrid once after a performance my host booked a table in a small charming family restaurant which stayed open a little later for us. My lady and I were treated like royalty and in addition everything tasted so perfect. Yet what of course adds to a meal is the service, and we were served by an elderly waiter who attended to our needs with such care and affection that I was as much moved by him as by the food. This older man was waiting to go home and I thought of the years he had slaved away for his greedy customers until he could return to his probably simple lodgings. His face had such dignity and decency I can never forget it.

Preface

Some restaurants have moved me to write about them mostly eulogising and others more critically. Yes, I am afraid I do identify food with love since it came from love – my mother's love – and I have been looking for love ever since. Even if it's just a simple desire to please and be proud of what they do. Restaurants are also a theatre and we are the audience being fed the drama, the food. And there can be good drama even in the humblest café.

JOE LYONS TEA SHOPS

It was home, a little piece of England that ma introduced me to as a child, and I'm pretty sure that it was in Luton, a town in Bedfordshire, where we were evacuated courtesy of the war. Lyons was my first memory of a café and its distinctive style impressed itself on my young brain … the aluminium facing on the double doors and the triumph of metal as you progressed along the self–service counter, picking out your faves as you passed the little glass cabinets revealing their treasures. You dragged your tray along until you came to the cash desk, and there would be a giant streaming cauldron of boiling water which the lady would then fill your brown teapot with, or maybe you'd have just a cup. Once in the big city I recall a sign there boldly stating that it was the best cup of tea in London and, of course, you had no reason to disbelieve it. It was dark and strong and, in fact, did taste like real tea before joke

My Life in Food

tea–bags took over. I think it was Lyons own imported brand.

Naturally there were the usual working or lower–middle class dishes that were the mainstay of its faithful clientele but closer to my heart were those savoury snacks, those small portions of food that a juvenile taste could become fixated on. I did develop a curious obsession for some thick red gunge served as tomato soup, and since you could help yourself I filled my soup bowl to overflowing. Later, when at school in London's East End, I would take my lunch at Lyons in Commercial Road and to my soup I would add dollops of the most delicious mashed potatoes, they blended together into a heavenly mushy concoction. No tastes could have satisfied me more and thus began my education in the arts of high cuisine.

In little glass cabinets were assembled a vast range of delicacies to which I found myself also addicted. Although these were just plain standard post–war foods, once they were chopped and assembled in these little dishes they took on an altogether different hue. You could have egg and tomato salad, egg mayonnaise, and salmon mayonnaise, but my particular speciality was potato salad. This comprised of diced potatoes in a Lyons' mayonnaise which tasted like nothing else on earth; it was that special Lyons' flavour, unique to that establishment, that had me hooked. Lyons also did a pretty show–stopping spaghetti on toast which tasted like nothing you would ever discover in its land of origin, it had been perfectly adapted to the bland

Joe Lyons Tea Shops

English tongue, and again it had that compelling flavour that seemed to draw you back to it. Ma liked taking me to Joe Lyons and it must have been a break for her from the tedious housework and constant cooking and washing. And so without any malice of forethought she turned me into a Joe Lyons junky.

Joe Lyons definitely drew people including the lonely and the dispossessed as well as the mums and kids who just wanted to take the weight off their feet. For some it was a sanctuary where you could sit and natter the hours away and nobody would even dream of bothering you; the nippies (as the waitresses were fondly called) nipped in and out dressed in mandatory black and white. They became as famous as bus conductors who were called clippies as the press seemed to bestow these diminutive but affectionate titles on those public servants who somehow got into the hearts of the country.

Old people sat and ruminated and the young gathered like hyenas round a water hole. In London, I next became familiar with the Lyons adjacent to Whitechapel station where nearby I had found a Saturday job as an assistant for the Pen King, a man who sold the first biros to be seen, this was also my first introduction to the world of commerce. After doing his spiel and working full out, my first taste of showmanship, he'd relax in Lyons for 20 minutes and leave me in charge of the stall. I was simply dying to make one or two sales on my own before he came back, but without his spiel it was impossible. Nevertheless I

My Life in Food

was deeply impressed that he left me alone on the stall, trusting an 11 year old.

On the wall of the shop was a large print of thin, strange–looking people, masses of them in front of a factory; I assumed these were factory workers and the picture always fascinated me. Of course, it was Lowry's matchstick men paintings and thus I began to develop a taste for art. Some enlightened being in the Lyons organisation thought it might be appropriate to adorn the walls with a subject that would have an emotional appeal to its customers. For some reason I found myself rather drawn to these helpless factory slaves assembling for yet another day of slog in some ghastly northern town in England.

In some ways Lyons was us, a bit of England a home from home, it was safe, functional and the food, modest like us, fairly conventional and reasonable. It symbolised the common folk of this nation. So we felt most comfortable in there and sat happily scoffing our simple but tasty portions watching the Formica table tops being swiftly wiped clean by the nippies, the low buzz of voices kept up its drone for most of the day. Also, they were usually spacious and quite elegant in a kind of Art Deco style with large mirrors on the wall. No other café chain even came near since they didn't possess the principles or the philosophy that seemed to guide Joe Lyons. Wherever you might land in London there would always be a Joe Lyons nearby, of course you would avoid the others like the plague and they soon fell by the wayside. However, as I grew older,

Joe Lyons Tea Shops

and peoples' tastes were changing and becoming more adventurous, London was besieged with a veritable plague of cappuccino cafés. Lyons seemed to fade a little. The tea shops were dying and the once proud standards began to slip, as if they too was reflecting society itself.

Later on I seldom visited old Joe's but sipped froth while reclining in raffia chairs surrounded, for some reason, by bamboo. Once, on a rainy day, I dashed into a branch of Lyons opposite Tottenham Court Road tube, just for the tea this time and a rest, and noticed that by the section serving tea and coffee was a giant open sugar bowl into which the world was dipping their spoons and the sugar had started to look grubby and even lumpy. I thought that this was it. The rot had started. I had never seen this before, and what a shame. However I still had occasion to use the tea shops and there was one in Little Newport Street next to the Arts Theatre which had been adopted by the acting profession. My friend John Dunhill used to call it pro–Lyons. There, mostly unemployed actors would gather to gossip and pass hints of who was casting what at the Beeb. As in those days the BBC was another benevolent organisation that was actor friendly and used to do plays! Now I was beginning to notice a new kind of clientele invading Lyons, almost as if it was being eaten slowly away by termites. The café attracted a type of grungy male hustler class – opportunists, part–time salesmen, grafters and conmen – who would sit in there all afternoon, yakking away, plotting cheap schemes and when not doing that burying their heads in the *Evening Standard* for racing forecasts. This branch was in danger of becoming a doss house as the fags burned in the ashtrays and a sour air of hopelessness pervaded the place. This one was one of the first to go. In its dying throes Joe Lyons desperately tried to reinvent itself by opening a series of American–style Wimpy bars which served the most amazingly tasty hamburgers, small but utterly delicious. This seemed to swing them around for a while but that too started to wear thin. In its heyday it was England and could not be anywhere else since they carried and imparted an atmosphere which was the essence of England. It was as English as Charles Dickens or George Orwell, something well–made, unaffected, and even rather original. Nothing really has replaced them in my mind, because the same spirit that created, patronised and supported them has, sadly, eroded. The society is perhaps not the same and so I miss you Joe. 'The best cup of tea in London.' And yes, I think it was.

TOMATO

Such a comparatively innocent rotund fruit – red and glowing in its abundant glory, blushing with rude health, silky to the touch – firm and almost bursting with joyous anticipation of being bitten and releasing its juicy promises. A jewel of a plant, also known more regally as *lycopersicum esculentum*, whose origin began in the steamy forests of South America. Known also as the love apple since it resembles a human heart. Its odour when natural is of earthiness and grassy pungency, weighty, with its liquid treasure packed within a delicate membrane. Sometimes bulging out as if it could not contain its ontological joy, into waves of flirtatious cheekiness, exulting in the sheer pleasure of being, gushing into your mouth as you tear it open with your teeth, as if it had been waiting and living for this moment of divine release, practically exploding onto your tongue. The simple humble tomato, the

My Life in Food

most flexible, adaptable, unique fruit that has shaped itself to all nations. It serves to enhance, exaggerate and flatter any dish that you make, will never argue or conflict with, but reinforce, stimulate and make better. It will, as a love apple, seduce any recalcitrant and bitter taste into a yielding and sweet–tempered dish. We love them so much that we like to preserve them in great jars from Romania, where they have perfected the art of pickling them, or we will dry them in the sun and call them sun–dried tomatoes, and mix them with olive oil. We capture their essence in purée for the pastas, or squeeze their rich liquor out of tubes – we will never cease to experience that twinge of satisfaction, the expectation as we hear the contents of the pot sigh in delightful appreciation as the red soft mulchy paste covers the dish in a roseate veil.

So the precious yet humble tomato, known familiarly as *tommy* will, in essence be our national fruit or vegetable since it has long made that leap into the other genus. No breakfast can really be said to be complete without its scarlet, reassuring rotundity sitting on the plate, half grilled, skin blistered or bursting on a working man's breakfast dish … The ghastly fatty, heart–clogging British breakfast with its over–salty, acidic bacon and pale eggs would indeed be a bleak affair without the comforting sun as its soothing companion.

Acting also as nurse, it will attempt to break down the fatty deposits clinging to the arteries of the carnivorous glutton, and thus it has been revealed to have supernatural medicinal qualities. Is there no end to its miraculous achievements? One scientist claims that its anti-oxidant properties frustrate the vicious cells in the male's prostate gland, coincidentally the organ of love, while another scientist has captured its DNA in a pill given the name of Lyc–O–Mato, a treatment that holds a total of six *tommies* in each of its pills.

But dipping into ancient memory, I first became acquainted with *tommy* when still in knee-chafing short pants, and surviving through those slim war-time years. Children seem to have an instinctive knowledge of what is good for them, since at this stage they are closer to the inherited instincts of their primitive ancestors, and violently reject what is not akin to them until they are bullied, cajoled, and give in to parental oppression and severely bad habits, which they pay for tragically in later life. But one day, ma gently fried up some tomatoes and laid the runny, pulpy concoction on to a piece of toast. Well, never did joy awake such pleasant sensations on my young tongue, that was still a virgin to the taste of the flesh. But now, oh heavenly, both sweet and piquant, a sharp yet vibrant taste delicately lingered on the tip of my tongue, as if reluctant to leave me. It soaked up the toast, which never tasted so happy, since as we have said, the tomato seems to bring out the best in everything on this earth.

And so, in Luton, a town famous for some reason for its hat industry, tomatoes on toast became the *sine qua non* of my young life, and no matter where I was, whether in school, with relatives, or endlessly playing in those park playgrounds, which were everywhere then, I would be comforted by the thought of what I could expect when I got home. This seemed to please mum no end, since the poor woman was in fits of frustration and despair, having cooked up some perfectly reasonable dish in her eyes, but in mine a concoction from hell, smelling of the charnel houses and sewers, from which I would run and lock myself in the bathroom. Even the overpowering stench of cabbage would make my young, innocent nostrils flare up and cause me to gag. Until one morning she happened to throw some tomatoes into the pan and my mind said yes, yes, yes, and I wanted more, more. Each morning was greeted with *toms* on toast and a *tommy* in my salad sandwich. I believe that coming from the monkey family and sharing their characteristics, we are really all natural vegetarians, devoid of flesh–tearing claws, and possessed of nut–peeling nails. I grew and grew, and red *tommy*–like cheeks could be seen on my face, which up to then had been a shade of sallow yellow. I grew, and one day left the nest, but never lost my fondness for those early jewels, and in remembering ma, I would associate her with a big plump tomato.

Nowadays *tommies* are treated with far more respect, even allowed to ripen and linger on the vine when they are sold, as if they had just been picked, especially in those smart new gourmet shops. I am quite partial to see them like that, splayed out like precious stones on a necklace. Now we see tomatoes in all shades and types and I am particularly drawn to the plum tomato, shaped more like a mini–torpedo, and the small, tightly packed cherry *tommy*. I nestle my nose into the cool satin cluster, and there is that smell again, a green, peculiar aroma, childhood rises up, and I'm once more sitting in our little kitchen in Luton, at home with ma.

CHICKEN SOUP

Perhaps there is something in the legend after all, regarding that famous stalwart of Jewish culinary life, the humble chicken soup, that for years we paid homage to on endless Friday nights with ma and pa. It soothes, it comforts and sustains and, for many believers, it is credited with mysterious properties of healing. Nevertheless, whatever science may discover of its medicinal powers, the simple bird united the scattered race somehow as we sat hungry and expectant, waiting for the golden brew to be set before us. Usually accompanied by a couple of miniature cannon balls resembling dumplings, and on the side a plate of crackers known as *matzos*; the unleavened bread fortuitously, if accidentally, discovered in the dash out of Egypt. So the ritual begins and stays in the mind as a symbol of unity, a rite seemingly centuries old, when in the ghettos and *shtetls*, and villages of Russia and Poland, the chicken

Chicken Soup

made its appearance every Friday night.

Once the Jewish symbol was the lion of Judah, but in exile it became the chicken of the *yiddeles* and, where once we roared and conquered, now we clucked and kvetched. In some instances an unkindly observer might even deduce a certain similarity in the thrusting neck, curved beak, sidelong look and excitable screech. Howsoever that might be, with the return to Zion many of these characteristics became ironed out in the turbulent gene pool of the races. Also, interestingly, chicken soup is not that easy to find in Israeli restaurants.

Mum would bring the golden elixir to the table. She had been so carefully preparing this as her mother taught her, and as she had been taught, and by their mothers of centuries ago in Odessa, when grandma would buy a chicken at the local poultry slaughterer, probably choosing some scraggy bird, still living and blissfully unaware of its role in Jewish society. She would wait for it to be dispatched and probably de–feather it herself in the backyard. Such was the way of life in London's East End when, even as a child, I would submerge myself into the tumult of smells and colours, shouts and cries that used to be Petticoat Lane. And in later years, when in possession of a camera, I would make my pilgrimage and think no subject more beautiful than a poulterer at his or her trade, hands coated in gore and proudly smiling.

Just off Wentworth Street there was a slaughterer's shed, and the first thing that hit you was the pungent stench of chickens, and the frightening whirl of a machine end which, since I was forbidden to peek in, I assumed was an electric plucker. All this made the event strangely macabre, and yet fascinating. Blood and guts on the floor, and feathers floating in the air. Some East Enders used to keep the bird in the backyard, where it would just peck all day long at some grit in between the cracks. So it was for a people deprived of land for centuries, often forbidden from owning it, the chicken became the most convenient beast and could be raised in your own humble shack, almost like a member of the family. Thus the chicken, merely an also–ran in the vast cornucopia of carnal delights, and hardly even mentioned in Exodus, became, during the Diaspora, a star player, elevated almost to mythic status. So this strange ungainly beast became the symbol of the race, its nourishment and weekly joy, and from such base and ignoble origins the humble clucker is Midas–like turned into gold, a golden sea of soup ladled out on Friday night to commemorate the Sabbath no less.

Ma told me that she had to buy a broiler and not a roaster, although such aesthetic deliberations tended to go over my head somewhat, the gist of it being that the broiler was more suitable for the soup and for the pot. Instructing me in the mysteries of the kitchen as if I were training to be a chef, she would instruct me to keep a vigilant eye on the pot and speedily scoop off any sign of what she called scum rising to the surface, and so what was left was clean and pure. Into the pot she would add the usual medley of carrots, onions, a tomato

Chicken Soup

and some herbs, and magically it would proceed to do its business. Separately she would prepare the *matzo balls,* or dumplings, or *knaydlach,* but the secrets of achieving rotund harmony and taste always evaded me. Or I couldn't be bothered. The Friday night rite began with a sliced bagel or two, lathered in cream cheese, and then came the star of the evening whose flavour was unvariable, always delicate, delicious, memorable, and some loose tiles of pasta could be seen floating at the bottom. Jewish penicillin, and for what reason we could not be sure, but rumour had it that it contained strong anti–oxidant qualities.

Naturally, as with all other races, immigrants bring their customs with them, and the soup has travelled the world. In nearly every decent diner in America, from the small town to the major cities, you will find it on the menu as a staple. I have pursued ma's flavour throughout the world, with a zeal worthy of Tristan when sent by the king to find the owner of a long golden thread of hair. From Goldenberg in the rue du Rossier in Paris to Katz's Deli on the Lower East Side in New York, I have made my quest and though finding simply delirious concoctions of other delights, the chicken soup evaded me. The reason being that so much else was available and the bird had lost its star status to the beef that was now freely available in vast sandwiches designed for crocodile mouths. I tried the Second Avenue Deli, and the renowned Carnegie Deli in Upper Manhattan, but to no avail, ma beats them all hands down. Of course, it's the devotional care

My Life in Food

that few delis can afford to give. My quest took me to Los Angeles, to Canter's, the famous 24–hour deli on Fairfax Avenue, which I imagine is the nearest to Jewish heaven as there can be. A sanctuary of a deli, a nirvana with a menu the length of the book of Genesis, with every flavour of the Jewish world and, as you stepped out of the blazing Californian sunshine into the cool cocoon of deli land, you stepped into a lost empire. Deli is something that paradoxically you cannot *fress* (eat) in the open air, not really. Canter's made do with a clear soup in which sat a giant matzo ball. Satisfying, but not quite what we had in mind. Even the famous Wolfie's in Miami could not compete. As each city loomed up into my life, sweeping around my feet like autumn leaves, I searched their streets for signs of deli. Friends sensitive to my never–ending obsession would recommend so–and–so in Toronto, or some other in Washington. With each visit my spirit rose and fell, and even the famous Bloom's of London's East End was sorely disappointing. Nevertheless, I would still search out some back street deli in Santa Monica, gurgling down gallons of the soup, hoping to find ma, or her spirit, within the golden molecules.

Years passed, and a friend told me of a deli in St John's Wood called Harry Morgan's and for some time I did satisfy some of my yearning with its tasty brew and first class dumplings. That was a good feast, but for me it was a slight *shlep*, the horrors of the nouveau riche, plump kids and the shriek of mobile phones were a deterrent.

Chicken Soup

One day, feeling ever so slightly down–at–heart since I was suffering from some as–yet undiagnosed stomach pains keeping me awake at night, I felt a call, almost an intuitive nudge to pull over to the right, park the car, and dive into a superstore. Swiftly and with no hesitancy, I scanned the shelves for an uncooked chicken, and only when I discovered a small organic corn–fed chicken did I cease my quest, bought it, and took it home. I would try to do it myself, yes, I would try myself to invoke the spirit of my ma in my own witch's broth. I eagerly seized the largest pot in the kitchen, filled it with water, brought it to boil, and then in it went, I threw in the rest of the vegetables, a dash of seasoning, and waited for it to cook … slowly, not to let it boil but simmer, and watching all the time for this effluent dark tide which I recall from mum's pot, but strangely there was none, just a watery soup very very slowly turning a pale lemon. I tried it, and not too much flavour yet, but hints of what was to come. I stroked and prodded it with my wooden ladle until it was soft and tender, and then lifted the poor beast out, cut it up, removing all the edible pieces, which were considerable in number, and chucked the carcass. Then I replaced all the flesh in the pot and continued to stir, season, taste. Very gradually, golden spheres of shiny fat floated on the surface, and the soup was beginning to look very ma–like. I tasted it … and yes it was getting closer. I let it continue to simmer very slowly, while I cooked up some Chinese noodles. These I added to my broth. I ladled it out. Oh bliss! For now that particularly unique and piquant flavour leapt onto my tongue, and I could detect her spirit in the taste, her ghost in the vapour. I had found the secret, for it was in me all the while, and she had shown me the way. After the second bowl I went to bed so content that even the pain in my abdomen subsided. Of course, the answer lay in the preparation, in the buying, the making, the watching, in other words, taking those same steps, one by one, was the answer. The art of cooking becomes a paradigm for your life and slows you down, makes you careful, thoughtful and inventive. The ceremony becomes a spiritual quest. I bottled the remains and put it in the fridge, and thus for four nights I celebrated. As I slurped down the golden brew I imagined that the spirit of ma was just hovering behind me, with just a gentle sense of approval.

HOT DOG

My ma called them Viennas and they were beef or veal frankfurters that she would slowly boil in a pot until one of the sides would split, then she'd fish them out and serve them with chips, though sometimes she'd put them together with scrambled eggs. They tasted even better when you pelted some OK Sauce over them and that would be a feast. After the war we had promised ourselves the ultimate goal of our lives namely to join our scattered family in America, New York to be precise, however I think that ma might have been too cautious, too questioning of everything over there that didn't compare favourably with our simple drab life at home, where we at least did have a small house of sorts and now we had just one room in an attic. Ma didn't quite take to New York, which under the circumstances was understandable. She hung back and didn't commit, without a husband to be there and fully

My Life in Food

support the move. I didn't see him searching for work or doing anything when eventually he joined us out there, except play cards with Uncle Joe in their front room. So there were ma, my sister and me living in the attic room on the top floor of a rooming house on East 173rd St which was at the heart of the Bronx. And I loved it!

I did commit, since it was natural – I couldn't help it … I dived into New York … I loved it, embraced it, explored my neighbourhood and found it so alive and alluring and went to school at PS70 in 174th St, it was all too wonderful and life was slowly unfolding its mysteries. But for ma, as with so many adults, life is just a stagnation from one crisis to another and she was stuck in that attic. I was in school discovering America and singing the school hymn in the morning *I Love Life and I Want to Live*.

When I went back three decades later I saw that the street had gone, that piece of the past, of history, people, lives, families, had been ripped out to make room for an expressway. But before it had been a long gentle, simple, nourishing street and right opposite my school was a deli. I don't now recall the name but maybe it was Nathan's, since that has a familiar ring, and their hot dogs had to be tasted to be believed. They were beyond wonderful. They were ecstatic, delirious, heavenly and homely and had that special and unique flavour of America. I imagine they were what you might call *kosher dogs*. They were 12 cents and they must have had such an impact on me that I recall them to this day, over half a century later ... remembering so clearly entering the deli, the counter on the right ... what the man said ... 'Coleslaw or sour kraut?' Of course I must have the kraut and I watched him carefully as he lined my dog with a stream of the pickled cabbage. They might have served all manner of things in there but that's all I ever saw or tasted, lined with that mild and unthreatening Yankee mustard. Now for me coming from rationed, plain food England, America obviously seemed to be a cornucopia of lingual delights and to have its own special taste, like taste taken to the limit even if some find it a trifle unsubtle. There is that soft, sweet, savoury, and compelling flavour that hits you in the face. The warm rolls, the hot frankfurter in that unvarying terracotta shade, the shreds of sour kraut draped over the length of the roll, the line of mustard resembling a wan yellow grin and then, ah yes, then you crunch down on that medley of flavours and you were immediately on your trip.

But ma got fed up and depressed and one savage winter's night we all piled in a yellow cab to take us to the pier where the stately Queen Mary was waiting to take us back to hell again. I was torn out of the guts of New York. The taxi had to be bribed since it was the fiercest winter New York had seen for 20 years. The grand and stately leviathan of a ship, the Queen Mary, mighty and majestic, stood in the dock and I quickly embarked and then just as quickly disappeared into the bowels of the ship. I had been rudely torn from the arms of my newly adopted mother and it all felt terribly wrong. The ship had its own comforting aroma of polish on brass and wax on wood, kitchens, laundry, sea, engines, but the crossing was rough and my days were spent languishing in the sick bay. Oh God, how small Southampton looked when we arrived in contrast to that stunningly dramatic skyline as you enter at dawn into New York. The East End was so depressing, God awful shocking, and my heart panged for my darling mother America. Everything tasted dull, there were compensations from the Jewish delis in the East End's Hessel Street, I did miss my precious hot dogs, but of course it was really what the hot dogs symbolised: freedom, 174th St, friends, New York, adventure, future, life! I had been able to see the Chrysler building from the school window when we were doing gym. Mr Rich, my teacher, was a kind loving man but I had been amazed at the laughter I had elicited from the other kids in the class when I addressed him as sir, as I would the teachers in my nice little school in Luton, where we had been evacuated during the war. I patiently waited and visited America many times later … in my dreams. I'd be walking through the city and I'd ask people how to get to the Bronx. I was so desperate to get back…

In our Bronx eyrie ma would occasionally send me down the street to the deli to pick up a few hot dogs to cheer her and my sister up since no–one was taking us out to dinner, I do remember that swift walk to 174th St like it's tattooed on my brain and so one day I did return. It was 30 years later and I took the subway

Hot Dog

all the way and my heart was beating in anticipation of reuniting with my past. I did see the old rooming house where Uncle Joe and Aunt Alice sat in the front room and played *Peg O' My Heart* on the turntable. All gone. Now the house was a builder's merchant but, on looking up, I can still see the attic window where ma would wave as I walked to school. And the school was still there but now the whole area was almost entirely Afro American where once it had been entirely Jewish, and sadly 174th St had been ripped out, my precious stream of life along with the deli on the corner opposite the school, now a wide dumb motorway. And who will mourn it? I will … I will always treasure that street and all who lived and worked and died on it. However, I did feel on this return a sense of reconnecting to my past … felt something reignite inside me, but then the mood gradually faded. I returned again and again to New York until I found work at the Public Theatre for the late and great Joe Papp. Oh yes, I was thriving in New York once again, and snatching back all that had been torn out of my hands and I was making up for lost time but now no more in the Bronx but in Manhattan.

One day, on 23rd St, on one of my interminable walks, the way one does in Manhattan, I discovered Katz's deli, situated on the Lower East Side in what was once the old Jewish ghetto. I examined it the way archaeologists might gaze penetratingly at the reputed tomb of Agamemnon. It had all the ingredients, signs of an East End deli. Slightly shabby on the outside

My Life in Food

and worn out, affecting nevertheless a stubborn cheerfulness in its advertising which welcomed you and, as if to prove it to you, had photos in the window of eminent showbiz or political personalities in frames, grinning happily with their arms round the owner. But something in the atmosphere had stained the photos and given them a slightly mausoleum look. In other words it was ghetto–ised. However, on entering I could see that I had hit the jackpot for this was the largest emporium of a kosher deli I had ever seen in my life … sheer deli–rium. Here was a carnivore's delight, a satanic pipe dream of flesh, flesh quivering in giant metal drawers where the Russian servers would take a chunk, stab it with a long fork and then shave a sliver off for you to sample before you received your giant handful of dripping sandwich. They'd expect a tip.

The families came with their fat wobbling offspring, their eyes glistening in anticipation of unbridled gluttony. At the entrance to the deli, as if occupying a slightly less important position, was the hot dog counter and yes, unbelievably they had exactly the same flavour as those that hit my taste buds all those years ago. In Katz's they just served you the dog in the roll and you helped yourself to all the trimmings from some large tubs with tongs to gather the sour kraut. You dipped your metal tongs into that crunchy barrel of kraut and crushed it inside your roll and oh … bliss and delight … yes I was back in America! And the taste! Having been without the taste for so long the impact of those flavours hitting my memory cells was indeed traumatic.

Hot Dog

I sat and devoured two of them, slowly, succulently and allowed the tape of memory to wind back to its beginning. My tongue has flirted with many seductive culinary bitches but there are times when food is more than a sum total of all its parts and represents something else and sometimes it's necessary to say hallo to your 10 year old self who apparently still occupies a place inside you and just longs to be patted sometimes. So I have to go to Katz's deli and for two dollars am fleetingly back in the 174th St with ma waiting for me to bring the warm hot dogs back but by the time I walk back to 308 East 173rd St they are just a trifle soggy. No matter. Still tastes good.

ROGG'S DELI

It's only just gone, just upped tent pegs and pulled out after 70 years or so on the corner of Cannon Street Road, London E1, and that narrow street that runs along the back to Christian Street, where my old junior school was situated.

Barry Rogg ran the small delicatessen for as long as I can remember as a customer, but before that I recall my ma going in, and there was always a queue, for it was renowned as the best deli in the area. A Jewish deli is wealth and riches and treasures galore. It is the source of the Nile, the core of food, the centre of the earth; it is the be all and end all, the alpha and omega. It is the cure for remorse, poverty, sadness, depression, sour weather, grief, and least of all a place just to stuff your stomach. When you bring the carrier bag home full of the goodies the smell is already pouring out of the bag and fresh and cold. The odour of herrings, olives

Rogg's Deli

black and greasy, snow–white cream cheese and tangy smoked salmon. All the varieties of pickled cucumber but the new green was simply the best, not the sweet and sour. The onions that came with the rollmops and fish cakes, the Viennas that you would of course eat with sauerkraut, jars of peppers salted and brined, the salami, sweet cheesecake, bagels and rye bread and on and on, so that when you shopped at Rogg's it was not an everyday affair, at least not for me. It was an event, a special time when the taste buds alerted you to their need for some soul food.

So when I was tempted by the newly regenerated Docklands to move back to the East End it was a bit of a shock to know that now I would be only just round the corner, more or less, from Rogg's. When I was a child I'd wait with mum in the queue and watch masses of notes, pound notes pass over the counter – since the Jews loved their smoked salmon, like it was manna from heaven, and would spend big money on it buying it flashily by the pound, which in those days was a fortune, while we queued and bought four ounces at a time. Ma always asked for the skin denuded of its meat, since that was free, and Rogg wrapped the salmon in it and, when we got home, oh my God, I couldn't wait to get my hands on it and chew the last remaining remnants; it tasted heavenly and even better than the silky coral slivers and, I must say, I did almost faint with joy as the cream cheese was spread on the bagel and the salmon laid over it … oooooow!

It seemed business–like to queue in Rogg's and

My Life in Food

that's how I always saw it; full of gossiping shoppers and a few busy men with businesses in the East End, homes in Edgware, and handfuls of money for the sexy pink salmon, a taste of gold, your symbol of wealth, your flavour of hope and happiness and salmon on the table meant that not all was lost.

So one day we came back to the East End and I went into Rogg's, run by the rotund son Barry Rogg, but this time there were no queues, no men clutching fivers and no busy counter hands slicing the king of fish. No, there was just Barry Rogg and his lady friend who seemed to assist him shyly.

The place still had that look, the look of a busy deli, the white tiles were still in place and the huge tin cans of pickles lined the walls … but they were empty and even rusted … yes, they were empty and even rusted and the shelves were full of these props and Barry didn't seem to care but accepted it as part of the décor since the food was still first class. But the shop was dying, just as the East End had slowly died, and was being colonised and fertilised by another group of immigrants who would come with their tastes, spices and food culture. Maybe some young boy will smell the food of his own Indian culture and weep for joy when in some distant place where he or she may have been temporarily deprived of it.

In fact we once lived opposite Rogg's when, for a few months, ma and I had to live in Cannon Street sharing one dull room since we had no home for a while after returning abruptly from New York. I would pass

Rogg's Deli

by Rogg's on the way to school in Christian Street. Each morning a fishmonger would ask me to buy a canister of tea for him and give me the empty tin jug to fill. He gave me two pence which was very welcome, and on I walked to Christian Street School.

Just up the street and off Commercial Road was one of the strangest thoroughfares I had seen in my life called Hessel Street. It was a fascinating narrow street that seemed almost to be torn out of the heart of Warsaw. Every single shop was Jewish or, even more, Yiddish and the chicken sellers had their wares hanging up, they looked so thin and scrawny but they reassured the customers that they were kosher. Along the dense tributary, voices cackled day and night and bagel sellers sat by their large sacks of bagels every few yards. It was intense, warm, vibrant and ever so slightly mysterious. Rogg's was at the end of this. Alas, Hessel Street is no more and not even a trace left of what it was, since brutal and unimaginative town planners tore down those marvellous old Dutch–style buildings and what is now left is defunct and quite horrible. For a few years I went to Rogg's and chatted and passed the time of day and Barry liked to see himself as a character, something exotic from the Old World. His favourite word as you sniffed around the shop was 'keep looking' to make you feel you didn't have to rush but let yourself be drowsed by his exotic display of fish cakes and cheesecakes and long hanging salamis but, to tell the truth, I didn't quite need what I saw as much as I used to. He would plunge his naked arms into the pickle barrels and fish out a few for you and while they were undoubtedly delicious the proximity of his being in such close conjunction was a bit intimate ... But isn't this how it always was and have we been too cosseted and spoilt by the immaculate presentation of supermarkets?

Rogg's was earthy, lively, and a throw back to older days. I went there less and less, but still tried to be friendly since Barry was at least some real and warm–blooded connection to my past and loyal to his old customers. One day I thought that the shop must surely die since no health authority would tolerate those picturesque and rusty old tins some of which were already anointed with cobwebs. But a strange thing took place, since Barry had repainted the place and refurbished it somewhat and now there was chance that he would be rediscovered by the new Dockland yuppies! They were beginning to change the area and several times I saw them, earnest, keen flushed faces sniffing, picking at the old Jewish delicacies and boldly buying two ounces of salmon and maybe even some fishcakes and being given the old East End patter by Barry before returning to their Thameside lofts with their little bags of tasty goodies.

This went on for a while and did furnish Barry with a slim income for a while, he continued to make most of his wares and no one on earth could better his fishcakes. With what enthusiasm he welcomed me should I by chance wander in when he had just finished frying them and they were hot. How he would pounce on me with eager exclamations of joy, encouraging me

Rogg's Deli

to buy some since, as we all know, nothing on earth tastes quite so fantastically delicious as a hot fishcake – especially his.

Over the years Barry never seemed to change even in his looks or his clothes for I could swear he always seemed to have on the same woollen sweater spread over his ample gut, and funny woollen hat, but equally retained his good humour and never once moaned about the demise of the area or loss of trade. Even in the bitterest of winters the front doors were open and the goods piled up high to the open doors. We'd exchange our usual pleasantries and he even went to see a show of mine. I was quite impressed since he never ever asked if there were tickets going but just went himself with his quiet girlfriend Angela. Sometimes the cat came out and jumped on the counter and Barry would feed him some salmon scraps. Anyway, cats are as familiar to Jews as they are to witches. They become like familiars.

But now, sad to say, I would drive past Rogg's since I could no longer bring myself to go in there. The last time, while he was cutting salmon, the poor man gave himself a small nick, nothing serious, and wrapped some tissue round it, and as he was cutting I saw the white tissue slowly going pink and suddenly I felt for him, for the hard life in his shrinking pool of clients.

So I drove slightly guiltily past and never failed to glance in but rarely were there customers anymore. Sometimes a neighbour might be in there just chatting away and the shop became more and more a strange deserted set, like a film set where nothing really was real. It should have been transferred lock and stock to the V&A museum since it truly was a masterwork. It seemed to contain the culture of centuries. Fortunately I have photographed it and I am proud of that. Rogg's eventually had to close, he invited a few people to celebrate and share a glass of wine, so we did and spent a few minutes with consolations but I think Barry was happy to go and may have done a good deal for the property. That shop was part of the Jewish world for three quarters of a century and is remembered by all who lived and died in the East End and is known to those intrepid wanderers who fled to America, Canada and South Africa. Rogg's was part of our lives and while it had to vanish we were also sorry to see it go since it was the last deli in the East End. The very last one to go. Alas, there are no more. Now we have Nobu!

THE BAGEL

The beigal (bagel) has long entered the food culture of the world, and has even become somewhat of a symbol – 'game as a bagel' – an expression I first came across in hard man, ex–bank robber John McVicar's compelling autobiography. It was rather disappointingly set to screen in the late seventies, with yours truly attempting my first villain in the shape of the notorious Charlie Richardson.

The bagel is the universal currency of many nations and has recently taken root in England on the grand scale of things. In my childhood it was confined strictly to the ethnic group from whence it emerged. One might proudly reflect on the considerable contribution the Jewish race had made to the world, chiefly characterised by great men like Freud, Einstein and Jesus, but one should also consider our proud little bagel. Quite an achievement. To my mind, when placed amongst our

My Life in Food

crowing achievements from relativity to psychoanalysis, the bagel is the crest, nay even the Everest, since it has entered every home and every stomach. The common bagel symbolises the philosophy of modern thinking; a fashionable invocation not to worry about trivial things becomes, 'think of the bagel and not the hole.'

So where does this intriguing idea come from? Who thought of making a roll with a hole in the centre? Does it represent some astrological black hole twisting snake–like through space, or the giant circular tunnel where matter in the shape of pulsars and quasars are hurled at frantic speeds in order to find even more minute particles?

But apart from the unique shape it is the flavour that really defies description as it is unlike any other bread and has the peculiar property of tasting subtly different on each bake, since the dough is twisted into coils after having been boiled, and then is finished in the oven. Indeed, on the occasion of picking up late–night bagels in Brick Lane, one might chance to witness at the back of the shop sinewy men with coils of dough, appearing almost to wrestle with them in the manner of that great Greek legend Laocoön, where we see a Herculean figure wrestling with what seems to be a giant anaconda. At that time of night the bagels are still warm. The flavour of a warm bagel is sensually delicious beyond all expectation, and so it is best when warmed and the butter melts over the crisp crust and soft spongy dough. Who needs gourmet?

The bagel was the link in a vast chain that connected

the Jews throughout Europe and Russia, and I am sure the medieval ovens were turning them out. When I was a child we lived, for a while, in Anthony Street in London's East End, and there was at that time a grocery store at every street corner where you would go and get the morning bagels. I would run to the shop and collect half a dozen, which curiously had the effect of cheering us up somewhat. We had a lovely little kitchen overlooking a tiny backyard where we would play, sharing the space with some grumpy chickens. At night–time, the sofa in the kitchen would miraculously turn into a bed, so you can see how convenient it all was. It was aptly called a put–u–up. In earlier years Dad would bring home the magic rings to our country exile in Luton, where absence of such savoury delights made them all the more intensely special. I still bear the scars on my thumb to this day from too eagerly slicing the damned things.

We moved eventually from our East End sanctuary to the luxury of a flat that even had its own bathroom! It was called the Woodberry Down Estate in North London, which sounded almost posh, and when I sent off for catalogues for self improvement courses, they arrived accompanied by fawning letters believing me to be the scion of some country squire.

However, being quite close to Stamford Hill, there was no difficulty whatsoever in obtaining the magic rings and after school, a miserable trip to Hackney, I would return home and devour six of the things just to put me in a decent frame of mind before supper.

Stuffing myself while watching a ten–inch black and white TV was as close to heaven as you could possibly get at that age. When I left school and even found my own flat, I would still make my weekly pilgrimage to the East End on Sundays, and go to the Prince of Delis, Marks of Wentworth Street.

Oh the joy, the intoxicating smells of old Europe, the sensual salmon so expertly cut, a tiny morsel extended for your approval. The gentle and ever–smiling Mr Marks (the younger) with his benign features and ever–ready smile. I would have to hold back the tears. However, sitting outside by his sack of bagels was a crumpled rumplestiltskin who was allowed to pursue his trade as a kind of appendage to Marks. A dozen bagels stuffed into a brown paper bag, usually quite crisp on the outside, but while I didn't mind them a touch firm, I didn't like them crisp, with occasional dark patches where the oven heat caught them, like they were mottled. I like them soft and the chewier the better. Years later Marks was reduced to half its size, and then it disappeared. A great loss to the East End. A legend dissolved.

Before this, and in my teen years, dad, after a night playing bridge at the spieler, would bring home bagels in the dark hours from some mysterious place, which always held me in wonderment since it was one of those apparent secrets known only to dad and taxi drivers. It also added to the mystery of my little seen and known father. One of those secrets of the night. Much later I discovered the Bagel Bake in Brick Lane, and after working at night in Greenwich in *The Glass Menagerie* by Tennessee Williams, I would have to stop off for the still warm bagels and drive speedily to Islington on my 250cc Honda motorbike trying desperately hard to resist the open bag on the passenger seat.

America, a nation which takes the ideas of the world and converts them into something after its own image, changes beigal to bagel, doubles the size, reinvents it, muscling up the slim Euro bagel, and flavouring it to a wild diversity for the ceaselessly unsatisfied and capricious Yankee palate. The flavour, the essence of what is bagel, is however still there – whether it be pumpernickel my favourite, sour dough, rye, egg, onion, sun-dried tomato – but never in this world could I tolerate the American predilection of trying to turn everything to infantile sweetness, hence cinnamon bagels. No. The bagel has to be savoury, and must taste of the labours of bread, and not the sweetness of idleness. Sundays with ice creams, or sweets for the lazy dessert. The bagel is stalwart, the original food of the peasant sold by the street peddler. It is unique in that it will try to improve whatever you put inside it. Never did smoked salmon taste so divine as when inside a bagel.

All over America you will find the bagel, especially in New York. On a chilly wintry morning, when the east wind carries icy gusts from the river, I would walk to Union Square and stand at the counter of the Bagel Bake, warm myself up, stare gratefully and longingly at the endless variety of fillings; so professionally served,

My Life in Food

so profuse compared to our East End counterpart with its one flavour and mean fillings. In New York the bagel has become the musical, it's all 'tits and ass'. The counter hand eyes me up as an a possible alien: 'Er, a toasted bagel … ' 'What kind?' 'Oh, er, pumpernickel.' 'With … ?' I could choose chopped liver, fried egg, lux, chopped herring, cream cheese (low fat or full), salami, turkey, chicken, coleslaw, corned beef, pastrami, etc etc … So, grabbing a steaming coffee on my tray, I'd sit while waiting for my choice to come up, and dive into the *New York Post* with its salacious mix of gossip and juicy crime. Nothing better, a touch Orwellian, New York style. 'Your order is ready!' he shouts. I have been keeping an eye out for him between the headlines, and was watching as he placed a square of grease–proof paper over the bagel when he sliced it so as not to have his palm smeared as he pressed down, how thoughtful and hygienic, and then he cut the bagel through the paper and that's how it is delivered to you. Now two smiling half moons greet me, stuffed with chopped herring, in my fave pumpernickel. Oh yes, the bliss. I gingerly chew a corner and my taste buds leap to attention. These emporia to deli exist all over New York, but they do not exist here for some unknown reason, even with a bitesize Jewish population. In New York it was a way of life, and the Bagel Bake was even stuffing a few cops as well. I don't know why they can't seem to get it together here in the capital city of London, except for maybe one or two rather underpowered, almost reluctant delis that are mainly unknown.

The Bagel

There is an excellent bagel house in Santa Monica, California. I would pop into Main Street, where the café was decorated in the sepia colours of old faded photos, and where pictures of Hollywood gangsters graced the walls as if testifying to the seriousness of the place. We mean business, serious bagels with serious fillings! The place was elegant and super–hygienic, with crisp, sharp–looking staff. My mind could never obliterate the image in the Brick Lane bakery of a woman covering some pathetic salt beef with a paper bag to protect it from the flies. Hygiene of a Victorian age, and not much had changed.

A town without a bagel house seemed lacking, with something missing, or something torn out, expatriated. How beautiful must Jewish Warsaw have been before those beasts destroyed it. A bagel house used to tell you where there might be Jews, where they thrived and were content. Thus I am sure that York will never have a bagel house, nor Lincoln, since these towns were graveyards for Jews in earlier tragedies. Paradoxically though, strains of Jewish life are returning to Germany, the largest graveyard of all. Long may they thrive, indeed they are now regarded as a little exotic. Sometimes still when driving home, I feel tempted to stop at the top of Brick Lane and wolf down a cream cheese and salmon bagel, hoping I don't finish it before I get to my door.

WOLFIE'S

Of course there's nothing like it on Earth, it's the synagogue of the deli for the Jews of Miami and has been here since 1947. The faithful come for that familiar smell and taste of home and the deli is unique in that it unifies all. Jews from every part that were scattered like so much seed on the wind reunite in the promised land of the deli where every taste of mom will be satisfied. Since I was here a couple of years ago Wolfie's seems to have faded somewhat as the young and middle–class have not the same cravings as their parents for the familiar aroma of *shtetl*, ghetto and slum, and go to fancy white–walled Italian galleries where food is served, like a painting, with a twist of complementing colour and sharp–tasting, chilled wines from cool, dark cellars. Here food is served like a feast for carnivores: obscenely huge corned beef sandwiches cut in half revealing their great wedges of dull, pinkish meat held together by thin, soggy slices of rye bread, steam rising from the sandwich's guts like it had just been ripped out of a recently slaughtered animal. So you try to soften the impact by a little deflection of mustard, then ram in some pickle, squash the tile of bread back on the roof of beef and open your mouth for a terrible crunch. A bowl of soggy pickles sits on the table.

It is, like so much of Miami, constructed in art deco style to go with the paint–blue skies and velvet green of the local vegetation, pinky–rose dawns and purple sunsets. The counter is pastel green surrounded by deeper apple–green bar stools which sit like mushrooms atop strawberry–pink stands. The chairs surrounding the small tables are in two–tone pink and green. The large booths against the wall are in a dirty pink from wear. The ceilings in America are not thought to be very important – since who looks at the ceiling? Tiled in that familiar cream that is now carrying the stains of decades of diners whose breath, smoke, smell and heat has forever imprinted itself like nicotine stains on the fingers of a smoker. The corners of the squares, the stale corners of sandwiches, are beginning to curl up in agony. Maybe Wolfie's comes to life at night like Canter's in LA but during the day it is the deli for passing trade and for a large swathe of Miami's community of Jews, the older ones who have traipsed here for years, ancient crocks bent over like hairpins escorted by an equally ancient crock or a black maid. The old one is somehow indelibly the last vestige of ghetto life, a body

My Life in Food

that battles valiantly against the debilitating effects of a youthful diet steeped in schmaltz, lack of exercise and a devotion to the soul food of chopped liver and eggs, wurst and fatty chicken soup with lots of cheesecakes. Nevertheless she carries her racked, old body – a faithful adherent to Wolfie's where she will relive the atmosphere of the kitchen table and the music of the chattering Jewish tongue.

As if to order, as if to fulfil the stereotypical image which Israel has eradicated forever in its new breed of healthy and powerful Jews, we see here the manager waddle up and down, supporting his gargantuan girth, a veritable barrel, neckless, a round football for a head in which two dark eyes swivel as if they were the only really mobile part, checking the restaurant at far greater speeds than this huge girth could turn. It all seems to be part of the intense Yiddish past: stifling tenements, small rooms, smoking fires, screaming babies, dining tables surrounded by shouting card players, and the escape into food, this is the balm, soothing and calming as the chicken soup assuaging all ills.

The café staff seem to be picked from central casting as would–be extras in the TV series *The Munsters*, and have the slick, world weary, cynical air of working in a place where the food never changes. They cannot become creatively excited like a waiter in the Italian theatre of food who learns his specials like an aria for the day, singing the praises of a starter of arugula and razor shaved Parmesan cheese resting like snow atop a salad doused in balsamic dressing. Here no such music will ever enter or leave his mouth. Only 'One corned beef and chicken soup' and 'Wadya wanna drink?!' He works a territory bereft of the demands of youth, in fact which youth avoids like a plague, and where cynicism is the only safeguard against rejection and a lifetime's incarceration in schmaltz. There is an attitude of Yiddish cynicism based on hopelessness and 'You will never surprise me and so, what's new', since centuries of claustrophobic oppression cannot be wiped out overnight in air–conditioned apartments and wide avenues. It will gradually thin out with each generation but here it sits in a carefully preserved time warp. No glamour of Miami stops here, but crusty, creaky age, neurotic and obsessive needs, a body full of pills and now some nostalgia to wash it down. The manager is walking around with that strut that fat men have which makes them look a little important, from where we get that expression 'Don't throw your weight around', which is exactly what he can't help doing. His chin meets his chest and seems grateful to rest on it. His thick, black beard seems to add that touch of seriousness to the indulgence of blubber as if it might be begging some attention to its owner's *mensch*–like quality.

There has to be some absolutely determined reason why the aged, the broken, and the bulbous work these restaurants, apart from the sanctuary they offer our more nebbish brothers and sisters, for we do not have hard–bodied Italian waiters dancing around the tables, barely concealing their healthy glowing muscles beneath their crisp white shirts, nor cheeky pearly–white–toothed girls bursting with sexual vitality beneath their starched little white aprons. As the deli is a wonderful collection of the viands of history, a plaiting together of the tastes of ancient Europe into one coil of delicacy so doth it not also bring with it some element of the human, not that I want body builders and sexy babes taking the order for gefilte fish but I merely observe that for the real feeling of the Jewish deli we seem to have characters that have just stepped out of the Warsaw Ghetto.

True, I see one or two waitresses who come into view who are not so *tzekrochen* (tired–looking, a little worn) but now my waiter comes over. He is priceless and by no means is he Jewish either but once the mandatory style is absorbed you grow into the role. His gestures have become so perfunctory they have developed an almost ritualistic pattern. He flicks open his order book, speedily takes your order, 'Chicken soup, one coffee!' and snaps the book shut on the order like it was a lizard snapping shut its jaws on a tasty fly. He wears the traditional black waistcoat, white shirt and black pants, which apart from the shirt are stiff with the clues of his trade. Just as the painter's smock contains elements of every painting he has executed in the years he has been wearing it, so this man's trousers and waistcoat must have the encrustations of several thousand plates of food. In other words, they are really crusty! After a few days or weeks they can't get any filthier, as Quentin Crisp so wisely observes in his philosophy about his apartment. We pretend not to notice as if it all fits in with the colour and charm of the busy, tasty, eat–and–enjoy deli. The pain of the past leaves a legacy, the eternal shrug of 'Who cares', but I do care. I had the distinct pleasure of eating in a deli in LA recently that was a model of perfection combining great Jewish deli with the streamlining of the times we live in. But here it is still not so important. My waiter scuttles through the dining room like a black beetle and seems fleshless, like his hips have no arse on them and he is a collection of bones held together by parchment and the crusty waistcoat. His face registers just the faintest glimmerings of life and since it inspires even a little fear, I am excessively polite as if his filthy crustiness, his dead eyes, his obscene lack of flesh were combined to extract some almost unwilling admiration. I mean, this is a being who lives in Hell!

My chicken soup arrives and tastes wonderful, it hosts a matzo ball, some noodles, and is golden as it should be. But then I risked a corned beef sandwich, actually a half, allowed if you purchased a soup. It came looking unpleasant, a thick pink slab rolled up and put between two half slices of bread. They had not made a whole sandwich, cut it in half and saved the half for the next soup and half a sandwich, no, they had just grabbed a lump of meat and smacked the bread over it so it lacked that crisp, sharply cut edge that is part of the aesthetics of eating. I mean presentation is just as important as taste. It was steaming as if it had been microwaved and the bread was hot and gooey over what looked like some rather slimy meat, not helped by the fact that I never usually eat corned beef except

My Life in Food

when some atavistic pull takes me to a Jewish deli. I didn't like the meat resembling the dusty pink booths of the restaurant. I took one nibble only and my whole being, tongue, nose, touch and sight concentrated into one gesture of repulsion. This was not the great sandwiches of Junior's of Brooklyn, nor the great Katz's Deli in SoHo, New York, nor even Canter's in LA, let alone the famous one in the Rue des Rosiers, Paris since I have tried them all already, tried them all. So I looked at the perpetual art deco blue sky through the window to wash my mind clean of the horror. The crusty, fleshless waiter had gone, I felt for him but his image will remain indelibly fixed in my mind, as happens when a place loses its joy and energy, when it slides downhill and becomes decayed. He was a touch Kafkaesque, perhaps a cousin to Gregor Samsa just before he became a beetle, and might be a candidate for such a metamorphosis.

There is still a certain charm and a famous Jewish *chutzpah* about the endless menu. Yet it contains too many vestiges of the past and I was glad to escape to the fresh–painted, sharp–looking, youthful café on South Beach. Just as I was also glad, years ago, to escape from the soupy confines of London's East End.

SUSHI

It came to me in 1981, passing a sushi bar each day in West Street, London W1, a few doors down from where The Ivy was to open its doors. I was performing in my play *Decadence*, an exhausting, celebrated, and physically demanding comedy that was thrilling to play and was having an unexpected success at the Arts Theatre in Little Newport Street. So, one Saturday, after a matinee and just out of curiosity, I wandered into the elegant minimalistic surroundings to try something different. I had just over an hour between matinee and evening show. I entered rather gingerly, and sat at the bar, a black ebony, U–shaped counter, and was comfortingly impressed by the stark clean simplicity of it all, functional and spare, very Zen temple–like. Your place was set with ritualistic formality as if you were indeed taking part in a religious ceremony, a wooden place mat unrolled for your array of dishes. One dish

My Life in Food

for food, another for your sauce, and a smaller one on which to rest your chopsticks, which were then made of hardwood and inscribed down the side in elegant Japanese calligraphy. Sitting at the counter one could be in the stalls of the theatre, watching the Japanese chef create magic with his deft, swift–moving hands. And there he is, ready for you and waiting upon your order. Inside a glass case you can admire and desire the fish of your choice, the dead flesh of the sea world lay in front of you, tuna, salmon, mackerel, sea bass, brill, abalone, sea urchin, yellow tail, squid, octopus. How tantalising, all arranged in their little sections and ready to be sliced, rolled, grilled, patted, or even revered with rice.

I begin modestly, and order some tuna rolls, now known to me as *tekka maki,* and watch him carefully take a thin sheet of parchment–like seaweed, scoop out a handful of specially cooked rice with his immaculately clean fingers which he is forever washing and wiping. He spreads the rice as if he were shaping an artwork out of soft clay, adds slivers of deep red tuna and rolls the parchment in a wooden mat, giving it the firm roll–like shape, dips his razor–sharp knife into some oil, then makes a series of swift cuts dividing my roll into five little barrel–like segments and placing them like my winnings on my wooden dish known onomatopoeically as a *sushi geta*! I watch with keen fascination since the feast begins here, obviously with the eye, and then the tongue, and so this is the secret, and why you should really sit at the bar.

Sushi

I unroll my little hot cotton towel, my *oshibori*, wipe my hands and even my face since I too feel I must be clean for this event, to partake in the ritual, the celebration where the sea passes into me. Oh the taste, the first taste, strangely exquisite, and never shall I forget it, the fusion of seaweed and rice enveloping the delicate and delightful fish. Warmth arises in my mouth and I realise that he smeared the rice with an apple–green pasty textured mustard known as *wasabi*, a small portion of which sits in a little dish, and on the corner of my *sushi geta* are some crushed slices of pickled ginger also known as *gari*. I want it to take time and so must not rush things here since the sensation is so divinely unique, and I add some *gari* to my *tekka maki* and oh the sensations are leaping across the neurons in my brain and the chef looks at me for approval which of course with mouth full I give in small murmurs and moans.

He is now waiting for me to make the next choice before I finish so he can get on with the task. However as I cannot overindulge before a performance I decide on some plain *nigiri sushi*, those tongues of flesh sitting atop those fingers of rice, at my request he issues a swift and affirmative 'Hai!' as I if had made the ultimate right choice. I watch him as he takes a slab of pale amber yellow–tail, known as *hamachi,* it's like pinewood stained in oil, delicately he slices two slivers off and hands me the pair. My chopsticks, *hashi,* turn into pincers, I take up the morsel and bite it into two pieces so as to prolong the feast and never have I tasted

My Life in Food

anything so frankly mouth–wateringly delicious, such a moreish flavour, almost smoky, every so slightly oily, and so very smooth. Ah, what a heaven I find myself in with only one other customer on the downward part of the U–shaped bar. Oh what a feast before the strains of the evening performance. I finished off with two fingers of lipstick coloured tuna, shiny glistening red tongues also known as *maguro* and I was replete for now, although I felt I could have danced all night. I returned to the small Arts Theatre in forever dusty Little Newport Street, and told my acting partner Linda about my discovery … 'Japanese? I've never tried that … I must go with you next time.' The small elegant sushi bar became my home for the next 10 years, and each change of sushi chef was like a small bereavement to me until I got used to the next one, and he became my friend until he too wandered off. There was a giant lobster on the back wall and a list of dishes written in Japanese calligraphy on wooden slats. Its authentic nature could be judged by the fact that few western people came here and at night it was invariably filled with suited Japanese business men knocking back masses of the rice wine *saki*, whose effect seemed to make them see the world through the funny bone, for this I have no known Japanese word. There appeared to be some kind of club upstairs frequented by Japanese only, and I suppose this helped to subsidise the sushi bar which was invariably empty except for the few knowing stalwarts. I did introduce my friend, percussionist Ray Cooper, to its delights and then each time I visited, even if there were months in between, I would be greeted by 'Oh, your friend Mr Cooper was just in here!' Ray liked Japanese as much as I did, and found himself a corner of the bar where he could even eat quite peaceably alone.

In 1984 I drove to the city of my dreams, Los Angeles, and performed *Decadence* there, in some worthy little 99 seat Equity waiver theatre, just for the hell of it, but it certainly helped me break into the movie industry. The show went as well as could be expected in that dumpy part of LA, with overpriced tickets which kept the audience away in droves, but after work Linda and I would head down to the sushi bar, now alas gone, on the corner where Santa Monica Boulevard meets Melrose. That was really special and so much cheaper than London, and here I first became acquainted with California roll, since in almost everything America seems to inspire you go a little wild and become inventive. So California Roll was a thick club, a baton of a roll on seaweed, but with extras like avocado, crab, even Japanese red pickle, and this was really delicious. Now I was beginning to appreciate the delights of just eating *sashimi*, which is only the slices of fish with no rice which you dip into the hot green *wasabi* and flick with soya sauce then wash down with about two small bottles of very potent *saki*, served so tantalisingly in small thumb–sized china cups.

LA was littered with sushi and now it was the new exotica of America. Later I was to discover Sushi On Sunset, shown to me by my friend, the actors' agent

My Life in Food

and producer Hilly Elkin, who brought Ken Tynan's *Oh Calcutta!* to New York, and became quite famous for marrying Clare Bloom! Now Hilly is brash, bold, opinionated, colourful, and was agent for my friend the late Georgia Brown, whom I first met in 1982 when directing my play *Greek* in the Matrix Theatre in Los Angeles. All the ex–pats came out of their mansions in Beverley Hills, to smell once more the East End nostalgically, and the play won many local awards.

So Hilly became a friend, a small, sharp, wizened and mercurial character who was one of the sushi set, for these aficionados swiftly became experts in the complexities of sushi and always know a brilliant new sushi bar – although they were almost all restaurants, bar has stuck. He would take me to one in or around Hollywood, demonstrate his extraordinary intimacy with the chefs and order all variety of things that I had never imagined could be done with fish. I would of course never go near prawn, *ebi,* and it is known for the common prawn *kuruma ebi* to be eaten alive! Nor for any fish from the shell with their rubbery, chewy taste, as the instructions in the book of Exodus regarding diet had made an inroad into my young brain and seemed to make some sense. Also, like prawn, *awabi* a sea snail or sea ear so called because of its shape, can also be served live ... ugh! Poor *awabi*. So Hilly would expertly order all sorts of dishes, which would roll in one after another, and get royally shit–faced on saki, and then with his endearing habit, would go round the room relocating peoples' necks with a mighty keraack!

Sushi

When I more or less resided in that great old community at Venice Beach, there was a delightful sushi house conveniently right on the corner of my hotel, now so sadly disappeared since so many sushi bars flower and die within a short time. Opposite my motel across the roundabout was a famous sushi establishment which catered for the young yuppie crowd. So sushi had become synonymous with noise, shouting, vulgarity, and mobiles, like 'Hey and woow this is fun', and a more hateful place you could not wish to go, but America seems to have an inordinate desire to turn everything into fun. Everybody was laughing, shouting and the sushi chefs entered into this and all you wanted to do was escape. I did and to a most utterly delightful and calm sushi bar on the Main street called Sushi Palette, so suitably named, since sushi is indeed so much like an artist's palette, and the chefs are indeed like painters or sculptors. Here I would relax and even could write in my journal and by now I might try a few other dishes like hand rolled sushi, a cone of seaweed wrapped around the contents which might be spicy chopped tuna, sliced cucumber, and egg roe. Of course this is mouth ecstasy, but I would also be partial to eel which is cooked and served hot and bound to the rice with a belt of seaweed also known as *unagi*. Not for me either was octopus or squid, although I seemed to tolerate a sliver of crab in my California roll. I have measured out my life in sushi, for wherever I went in the world, I would search out the sushi bar, and at once find a certain quietude.

My Life in Food

At last I went to Japan to perform at the Saiyo Theatre in the illustrious Ginza district, and found the sushi is not the only dish in Japan, but one of many, and the most popular are soba, noodle bars where you can sit by scrubbed wooden tables in a small steamy café seating no more than a dozen people, and gorge yourself on massive soups, mini bathtubs of lightly cooked veg or chicken. Next I discovered the mechanical sushi bar which utterly astonished me at first with its brilliant invention of having your preprepared dishes circle the room on a conveyer belt until you have amassed a miniature skyscraper of colour–coded dishes. There is a brilliant chain now operating called Moshi Moshi sprung from the regeneration of Liverpool Street Station and the filthy squalor of *Elephant Man* and greasy soggy British food. A new world has emerged thankfully, and the sushi bar is a new experience where you can eat and watch the train departing beneath you to those ghastly British cities.

Naturally, sushi is also a very useful game to play with your new, as yet untried, lover, who may not be familiar with chopsticks and one of the joys of introducing her to sushi is that you are able to teach her, very gently of course, how to use the little wooden sticks, and guide her into the tastes, and so this can become a courting ritual, a delightful ceremony as you help your beloved like a child holding her first knife and fork. This often binds you even more.

Now of course, sushi has become high status since its inception, and the gradual decline of fish stocks means that the humble sushi, once the staple of the Japanese working man, has become elevated to culinary palaces in breathtakingly expensive eateries such as Nobu and its brother Ubon on the Isle of Dogs. On the other hand, the world has become sushified, and even supermarkets sell sushi selections of ghastly tasting scrappy sushi with mean bits of tuna in *tekka maki* rolls, and miserable flattened prawn, and nasty cheap scraps of fish. What was once the most elegant and delicate of culinary expression has become fast food! Nevertheless, I can say that I never enter a sushi bar and sit at the counter without a frisson of high expectation going through me. I recall when directing *Coriolanus* in New York in 1988, I would exit into the New York night since it was November, and the day would have mysteriously changed into inky black night without my noticing it. I would come out so relieved and stimulated with the progress of rehearsals and realise with a sense of euphoria that I was in Manhattan and it is exciting just to be out on the street. I would meet my ex–wife, Shelley, and wander across the road to a cavernous sushi restaurant, sit at the bar, sip some *saki*, roll a cigarette, order a yellow tail *sashimi*, talk about the progress, order another *saki*, order a rainbow roll, chatter, smoke, drink, eat, ahh, paradise. Thank you – *domo arigato!*

STEAK IN CANNES

I was sitting in my Brighton flat when my agent in LA rang and said to jump on the plane for Cannes. Terence Stamp had walked off a film that was to be directed by the famous pop singer Prince. I duly jumped on the plane and stepped into Terry's old clothes – Cannes was very nice. But as usual I found myself alone and reflecting on a piece of fillet steak.

Dinner last night after a late September swim was wonderful. I found the right corner in the restaurant – one has to be comfortable – a well-located seat with a good view. Not too near anyone. I ordered, for a change, *filet au poivre, haricots verts* and mixed salad. The tablecloth was coloured in pastel stripes and the head waiter deliberated in front of me, and every choice I made was 'Parfait', flattering me as if my judgement reflected the discriminating standards of a gourmet. I settled down with the evening, enjoying the succulent cool air washing over my tight, sea–washed skin.

The French bread arrived first, with the *vin* naturally. The *pain* was fresh and crisp, brown and crusty with a very moist interior that had the flavour of sour dough; I hate the texture of baguettes when they are dry. My half bottle of 1981 rouge of unknown vintage was uncorked, and I supped it, and it was only as French wine, that's bought and drunk in France, and in the South of France too could be … and in the open air at that. It tasted earthy, fruity and mild with no trace of that acidy tang you get in London when you are unsure whether it's quality or cleaning fluid.

As expected it tasted perfect, better than those expensive decanted wines at the Connaught – because you should drink wine in its original country and not in swanky restaurants in New York and London. No; they must be drunk, preferably in the open air, with crispy moist French bread on the Riviera, on an evening in September when your body has been washed in crystal clear waters and the night slowly turns from lavender to violet. Then it tastes … so I drank the wine of Burgundy and it slipped down very easily … like liquid earth.

I waited some time allowing my patience to be tested and stretched before I received my simple dinner – nothing fancy drowned in painful sauces but simple and wholesome, the obvious French dinner. At last along came the steak and it was 'Parfait', sitting there swaddled in pepper sauce and coated in some unknown ingredients like, perhaps, cream and herbs and of course peppercorns which have been crushed into the sauce.

In a separate tureen sat perfectly cooked *haricots verts,* just springingly lying there in heated garlic butter, and a salad tossed after careful removal of the sliced tomatoes onto another plate. The salad was robustly coated in a delicious French dressing and the enlivened and glistening green sheets were deposited onto the white plate. I took my well–sharpened knife and sliced the steak. It's blood runs free, raw as a wound, soft as a kiss. Well, not so much blood since I ordered medium rare, but delicious. The sauce in which I cradled my segment of meat had an almost malty as well as peppery taste, and was also sharp, yet was cushioned by the cream from attacking one's palate with too much ferocity.

I crushed it between my steel–capped molars and ground away with my incisors and swallowed it down followed by a cascade of wine. Parfait. It was hot and tasty and done just right, and the taste is mixed like the wine with open air and the soft luke–warm breeze. The meat hit a zone of memory and discharged a warm glow of earlier meat–eating times. Now I hardly ever touch it, but at that moment it gently ran along all those nerves and cells that eagerly responded and yielded to the furious embrace of protein. I sliced once more and revealed its pink centre and the *filet* didn't collapse after the first assault but still stood supreme and proud: dense packed meat. It was determined to stay crisp to the last slice. Seeing this apparent integrity relaxed me enough to lay my knife and fork down and survey the work. So unlike your British restaurant where the meat would already be collapsing in resignation with its forlorn state requiring – nay, even demanding – the constant attack of knife and fork so that the flourish of weaponry might disguise the tawdriness of the meat's performance. A good steak should preserve some structural integrity to the last slice.

Now it is necessary to survey the battlefield, to enjoy and feed your eyes while the stomach is busy sorting and identifying its new treasures. It looks good. I lean back and photograph it in my mind. Who needs company to interfere with this ritual? The steak was a third devoured. The remaining meat standing with shorn off side, not ragged but clean like a stone newly–broken revealing the perfect smooth core. For a moment it looks like the chalky cliffs meeting the sea at Brighton, but less crumbly, more like a side of Cheddar and the steak looks seductive as the tide of gravy gently licks at its base. It needs no co–star. The *haricots,* which are beautifully cooked, are transported to the plate and instantly dashed to pieces in a basting gravy and the fillet once more in its centre stage.

The restaurant, like a beacon of warm light in the twilight, is claiming its customers who sit wherever they are placed and fill up the little spaces like a crossword. A couple with a child sit at the next table and the nasty little brute keeps sticking her tongue out as if this were some kind of achievement and whom I ignore after a few retaliatory lingual thrusts … And now an older couple have the temerity to be seated right at the table next to mine. Well, in France people don't mind such proximity since eating rules communication. I decide to engage the salad in a little side distraction and pull out the larger leaf of lettuce which now resembles a piece of green velvet and the dressing is rich, garlicky with just enough mustard to make it interesting and attention–grabbing and a perfect contrast to the fillet … Before returning to my amour I nibble quickly on a torn–off fragment of bread, to absorb the slightest tingling on my tongue from the vinaigrette – just to make a bridge so to speak between the salad dressing and the steak sauce, not to confront them and create war on my taste buds. The bread kept the two adversaries apart in their more piquant extremities. I slice the steak once more and it's still holding on to its heat and I crush it with as much fervour and passion as the first slice when we met. This is a relationship that will not fade after the novelty of the initial excitement; in fact it is increasing and I eye with a certain amount of comfort the remaining sizeable portion. It will sustain further assaults and not be demolished. The wine is still oiling those rusty hinges and pleasant day–dreams are being released from the stump of memory.

There is something pleasant about being alone, if you do not gaze into paranoia watching the world holding hands and families chattering like monkeys. If you can be quiet and calm within yourself it is like watching a movie. The absurdity of human behaviour is undiluted by the diversion of company. The world seems like a madhouse and the more trivial aspects of human beings are viewed in sharper focus. Here, now, the dinner is my companion and ally … my sole joy

Steak in Cannes

and friend ... my only hope ... my restorative, my amusement, my art and, most of all, my entertainment. I watch a woman opposite chipping at a hard red nail and for a moment I ponder the need for these fingertips that seemed dipped in gouts of blood. It occurs to me that while the human body is subject to the ravages of time, the nail is hard and imperishable. It gives these women a sense that something within them is hard, firm and durable. For a moment I ponder the chef in the kitchen, since we never seem to think of them now, but I wish to imagine the backstage with its haste and preparation, its medley of shouts and curses. I turn back to my plate, my wine and my salad all grown for me ... all destined to arrive at this particular point in time ... all containing elements of the earth and sun. I finished the steak and I finished the dinner and, like an old friend, my companion for the evening rests in peace reconstituted inside me. I paid the bill. 'Ca va monsieur?' the head waiter routinely demands. 'Parfait.'

TEA AT REIDS

There are few experiences that one looks forward to with more unalloyed joy than tea on the exquisite black and white terrace at Reids Hotel, Madeira. Your backside cradled by the cane chairs and your eyes soothed by a bay of everlasting blue under a slowly floating carapace of soft white gossamer clouds. The tinkle of cups and saucers decorated with ivy leaves … white linen tablecloths edged in pink … the stone chessboard floors. Then let your eye wander down into the garden with its wild profusion of arboreal delights; pine, cactus, palm. One stately pine lifts its needles upwards as if it were a candelabra shooting green flames, and the white arches on the terrace frame the clouds over the harbour which miraculously never seem to come out this way. Tea is always taken at Reids at 4pm as if it is a ritual that will last forever, as long as Maderia lasts. The long dead who had taken tea at

Tea at Reids

Reids include King Umberto, Winston Churchill and Bernard Shaw. Tea is a time between the life and death of a day, between the fierce explosive nature of the morning to the gentle sinking of the sun. At the first dying of the day you take tea, which is so English and a time of memory and nostalgia, reflection rather than, as lunch or dinner, a time for absorption and gluttony. There is a photo in one of the many lounges of Bernard Shaw taking a dance lesson and the picture shows him being guided by a dance master and he has signed it to 'the only man who has taught me anything'. A white–coated waiter brings a menu, a folded card which says boldly Afternoon Tea and with a watercolour image of the terrace featuring an aquamarine sky, a table set for tea and shadows daubed in blue. The picture reminds one of a perfect sunny day between wars when holidays were intense with excitement and anticipation, like the pastoral British Railways posters with their trains puffing out pure plumes of non–offensive smoke, liquid blue skies and bulging cheeked suns … cotton dresses invited you to the blissful seasides awash with mirror–shiny haircuts. The air here is as pure as scented flowers. The wind so gently flutters the leaves and the great fronds sway lazily from side to side. The sky is broken up but soft and ragged with great expanses of the reassuring blue while the sea is streaked with indigo and purple, and distant clouds filter the sunlight. Atop Madeira's mountainous forest it is nearly always wet and grey, fertile, soggy and misty – but down here it is sun and light. The cake trolley summons your response:

a thin banana or an equally thin, delicate papaya cake. The multi-coloured sweet offerings beckon you to scoff but you want to retain an edge of hunger for dinner … most important.

Small East End Jewish grocers shop

East End chickens

The men of Bloom's, London E1

Breakfast with Clara in Reid's Palace Hotel, Maderia

Breakfast at the Copacabana Palace Hotel, Rio de Janeiro

Sliced tuna ready for sushi, Madeira

Fruit for sale, St Lucia

Waiting for lunch, Phuket beach, Thailand

Mezes lunch break, Accra

Breakfast at Hotel la Voille d'Or, Cap–Ferrat

Wine, vinegar and oil, Greece

Salad on the island of Skyros

Lunch time
Grand–Hotel
du Cap–Ferrat
France

Zara's famous grocer deli

Clara in
Katz's Deli,
New York

A bottle of wine, Cap–Ferrat

Elderly couple New York diner

Dining with Joan Collins during the filming of *Decadence*

CHURRASCARIA

Some years ago I was in Rio working on a bio–pic of Ronnie Biggs and he introduced me to a novel way of eating – at a Brazilian steakhouse called Churrascaria which means a way of cooking meat barbecued on charcoal. A meat house like no other. Here in Brazil everyone who can afford it eats meat with a vengeance. It is the staff of life. It represents the wealth of Brazil; the vast ranches and endless tons of meat that go through the stomach. Not for Brazilians the lean or *nouvelle cuisine,* or culinary pampering for neurotic, water–drinking designer vegetarians. Here meat is ubiquitous like the smog, wherever you go you smell the tang of roasting meat in the air, in the cafés, bars, butchers, on the street stalls sold on sticks and dipped in hot sauces, on the beach, in pasta, as an *apperitivo* in a sidewalk cafe where a group of people will share a dish of finely sliced fillet cooked with spring onions and spear it with toothpicks, in street markets sliced in sandwiches, and finally, the king of them all, the *churrasco*.

Here you sit and the waiter brings to your table every kind of meat from all parts of the animal, so you are not restricted to your rump steak and chips. First he comes and dulls the edge of your appetite slightly by offering you a salad plate, which includes the delicious heart of palm, soft and textured like marble. Then, like heralds bearing scrolls, the waiters enter with these long skewers of charcoaled meat which have been burnt fiercely on the outside and, when sliced, reveal the pink flesh underneath. So it has also a slightly erotic undertone, as if the delights were revealed by the slicing off of the overgarment. It's only salted on the outside; no other flavour used in the charcoaling except its own juices.

The waiter carries the skewer of sizzling meat in both hands while bearing in his lower hand at the same time a little silver bowl in which to catch the fat; not always successfully it would seem, since the floor of this particular café is like a skating rink. One waiter may again offer you a starter, like sausages or chicken, and if you demur another waiter is speeding swiftly toward you with a giant stick from which he will slice off a section of the prepared meat and swiftly return the shaved skewers of meat to the burning coals for sealing. You've hardly finished your slice when the waiter glides back with his sizzling rump or sirloin on its iron skewer, holding the other end in its metal cup. With a razor–sharp knife he slices it slowly from the

Churrascaria

top, the meat gradually falls away and before it ends up on your plate you are invited to spear it with your fork to prevent it slapping inelegantly down. A thin slice, darkly barbecued on one side and virgin on the other. Another waiter will come by offering kidney, liver and other delicacies, but you will safely remain with fillet or rump. It tastes unlike any other meat. It tastes supremely good.

I am plummeted back to my heady old meat–eating days, before conscience, ecology and additives diminished my desire for the red flesh ... when meat was wholesome to a growing child, like the slice of bread Mum dipped into the stewpot, then held out sopping and tasting more wonderful than anything on earth. In later years, living with and knowing vegetarians has opened all the doors of an alternative world of taste. Meat sitting in the fridge on a white plate onto which blood has oozed out was a thing of the past. That slightly sick feeling when you slice a steak and it's just too raw and you are inevitably reminded that it is blood which is leaking out, however much it is decorated with sauce and peppercorns and surrounded by innocent little sprigs of parsley, as if to help you reduce the slaughter on your plate. Here meat is and feels like sin, and makes no pretence of avoiding its role with décor. It's just plain meat.

The white–jacketed waiter approaches and you have never tasted meat so good. Its only flavouring is salt – they don't even serve mustard. And you don't have to send it back since it comes as raw or as well done as

My Life in Food

you wish. Ronnie introduced me to a good *churrascaria* and interpreted each offering, 'Try the lamb, this is the shoulder, and what do you think this is? Have a guess?' ... Could be turkey. He seems to know immediately each part of the animal – the shin, thigh, topside – introducing each one like guests arriving at a party. So now I can venture alone.

Offerings are now coming more quickly, before you've even had time to denude your plate – roast beef, turkey wrapped in bacon. The waiter skews off a couple of slabs and you get back into the act, washing it down with a good glass of the Brazilian national drink *caipirinha,* like a rum made from sugarcane, with lime, crushed ice and sugar. A chunk of mignon. The knife flashes and the meat slaps down onto your plate, with you obeying the ritual with your fork, guiding it gently down to land. The slices are not too thick – just sufficient each time to leave you wanting more. Its heady stuff. The pork's declined. No more chicken or sausage. This is certainly a place for serious indulgence and it needn't cost a fortune. Sometimes there is in all of us a desperate need to pig out, to indulge in some carnal offering, be it flesh, eaten or desired.

The knife again flashes through, and there is no inclined eyebrow by any waiter since this is what you are here for. The meat sizzles and the fires roar in the distant open kitchen. The smell is good and now I feel my waist pushing against my belt, so I loosen it, relax from the kill and look around at the other carnivores. They don't actually look too healthy, I force myself to

Churrascaria

admit. A man on the next table is so obsessed with his piece of meat that he is trying to swallow the whole slice and some of the meat remains outside his mouth hanging down like some disgusting tongue … I turn away promptly from the hideous sight … I glance at the other customers and see some solitary eaters like myself, but older, rich–looking men with yellow faces for whom company is a piece of dead meat being brought smoking to their plate. I begin to feel as if I am at a debauched gathering … carnal desire here takes on a new meaning. It's easy to eat since you never see a giant fillet steak on your plate, but only a slice at a time, and when it comes to your plate it almost looks like a piece of burnished wood. It looks too good to refuse.

You forget just how many slices you have had … six, eight, ten, twenty? The offerings continue to dance in and out of your vision. you begin to decline and slow down, and yet meat is the one thing you can still eat after real hunger has long abated. It longs for your bite, the taste clings to your teeth and I suspect you must be fulfilling or awaking atavistic longings … you feel bestial as you disturb some primitive appetite. I glance at myself in the mirror on the wall to check myself … Do I look evil yet? Gloating? Wolfish? I imagine that I would start to reveal signs of the sweaty, yellow demeanour of the compulsive meat eater. However I am disappointed to see I look more or less the same as when I walked in. Obviously it hadn't taken its toll, yet. I pay the bill, which comes to 400 *cruzieros* – a blow out for less than four pounds. I have feasted, if not with panthers, at least like a panther. A small puritanical streak in me makes me feel as if I have been to a brothel. A bit of an orgy, what?

HOMAGE TO GRANDE-HOTEL

Perfect breakfast on the terrace: a basket of rolls, croissants delicately crisp, overblown boomerangs that you anoint from any of the three delicious jars that sit on the table: *miel de France* (honey), *framboise* (raspberry), *Reine Claude* (plum). Each is labelled with a small picture of its contents – a bee, two raspberries, two round green plums – to enable foreign eyes to identify the contents of the succulent fruity pots. A rose plant sits in its terracotta pot on the mottled grey stone table, although it could be marble. Our table is set with rectangles of pink linen upon which are placed our china plates decorated with tiny floral motifs. I pull the tail off a croissant which tears with the expectant resistance of a pastry well baked, unlike their poor British counterparts, those soggy overheated corpses that hang limply like Dali clocks. Here the tail gradually yields itself and, after its baptism in *Reine Claude*, I pour the coffee which comes in a small delicate china pot with a leaf motif circling the neck as if it were wearing an emerald necklace and round its body little flowers are scattered. The coffee tastes earthy, brown and brackish, it flows into my vast dry and thirsty gullet while I'm being entertained by the birds' choral orchestra. Sparrows emboldened by the placidity of tourists over the years tweet and puff their chests out and advance to the basket of goodies ignoring the sluggish waiters' attempts to shoo them away. They stand on the edge of a bread basket, for all the world as if by long usage it were theirs, and peck away at the Cyclopean rolls that a customer has left behind. Or they stand at a distance and make piercingly sweet requests that you throw them a few crumbs.

On this morning, great rivers of coffee are being poured down the giant throat of France and a million or so croissants are being ripped apart, dipped into coffee, smeared with jam, stuffed with cheese or grilled with ham. I watch the great mantle of the sea down below our grand white hotel and am able to see the wide shimmering vast Cote d'Azure – as azure as the name, as diamonds twinkling, in varied hues of indigo, violet, fields of bluebells, deep aquamarine, cornflower and deep summer blues. The hot June sun bathes the coastline from Nice to Monaco. Saint Jean Cap–Ferrat is a thumb of land sprouting tree–shaded villas, sequestered roads that drowse like it is always Sunday. Avenues of pine, scents of sage, rosemary and lavender fragrantly mix with jasmine, oleander and roses. As you stroll through the odoriferous paths, plumes of other activities come sneaking into your alert nostrils as ladies heat their olive oil throw in garlic and lunchtime signals a whole new waft of smells.

Meanwhile I am still at breakfast and my fruit salad arrives brilliantly festooned in scarlet – bright red raspberries, dissected strawberries, yellow diced guava, amber papayas and orange segments, lightly splashed with the sweetened juice of pears. The birds chirp even more loudly, piercing the air with an excited naked lust for the food that they see laid out before them. So I tear off a fragment of croissant, which, after a few moments of trembling hesitation, is seized and chewed by a braver fellow, who doesn't even bother to fly away with it since it is not worth the energy, but merely sits on the edge of the table joining me for breakfast.

Now other tables are filling up with the sleepy latecomers enjoying the distinct privilege of opening their eyes on wondrous, ethereal sight of a new morning being born out of the moist blue mist. A German family, there are many here, adds another melody with their sponge tongues which sound like people drowning in swamps, scalded snakes or ships' foghorns or a combination of all, and they order heavy German breakfasts replete with ham and eggs. I drink the last of the coffee and gaze over the long line of the sea at the edge of the garden and imagine myself in there soon.

I walk up the stairs to our room that overlooks the sky, the leafy treetops and the sea, the tricolour of France through the window. I prepare for the sea and change into trunks, fill a bag with a mask so that I may peer into the mysteries of the depths, and grab a camera, towels, books, fruit, lotions, pen, notebook and rubber shoes so that I can stand in the water and not suffer a long urchin's spike through my foot.

We go through the garden, past the table where several birds are finishing my uncollected breakfast, through the gate at the end and down the arboreal, well-kept Eden leading to the sea and pool. We ignore the pool where the ancient ones are crawling slowly through the overheated, pampered and poisonously chlorinated water, past the limp bodies lying like melted wax reading glossy magazines reporting the inane activities of the world's junk, past the metal gate which takes us out to the small spit of rock from where I sink into the water that surrounds me like a caress. It forms a cool wet embrace round my body and gently licks at my skin with tiny wet kisses and, even without peering under the veil of the surface, I can see the small venomous-looking Medusas with their electric trailers hanging from their bodies like tresses. They pulse slowly through the water, a single organism or valve, pumping like a heart. Their shapes are formed by the water and they collapse like a squidge of jelly outside of it, but now, floating in the liquid blue, they resemble starships gliding through space and ready to burn you. So you carefully navigate a passage through them with your eyes open wide beneath the waves, scanning every movement while the ground slowly leaves you.

You have then an impression of floating over a huge Venusian landscape, as if you were flying through the land of dreams and where, without effort, you can leave the ground. Often have I flown in my dreams where people stare at you with astonished bewilderment. Now in simulation of this I float weightlessly over the watery abyss, above rocks and crevices, and ravines which stretch out into the vast distance – all revealed only by a snorkelling mask which exposes deep gullies, overhangs, and jagged edges of rocky terraces. The waves' giant paws gently try to push you against the rocks and so you must dive and go beneath the turbulence. From below it looks as if the surface were a huge transparent cloth that was being shaken out, a skin, a sheet billowing in the wind, while here all is soft and quiet, yielding, like gentle molasses. Striped fish swim in shoals, darting away as you near them, and linked in rhythm as if a pack of cards had been thrown in the air and descended in slow motion.

It is the last day that the croissants come, over the gardens the sea is misty and mercurial blue as the sun washes in from the east. A glorious explosion of swallows whipped past our sleepy room in an early cacophony of squeals, probably chasing swarms of flies. We walk past giant yellow flowers whose vast open trumpets are lined with dark pencil–like streaks, probably landing strips for the bee to hone into before it wriggles itself inside.

Purple bougainvillaea soften the corners of the walls, waiters dance in attendance round the tables in perfect

My Life in Food

imitation of the bees buzzing round flowers, and the coffee pours again down a million thirsty caverns. The birds cover the gardens with their song, while the sea gently washes against the rocks softened over millions of years, smoothed enough for the thousands of feet that have carefully stepped down into the sea that is as clear as glass and warmed by the sun. As I plunge in I follow a thousand shadows before me and as I sit with my orange juice I occupy the place in this wicker chair that a thousand other bodies have nestled themselves into and happily gazed at the silvery pastel–blue sea mirroring the sky dotted with speeding swallows. They too opened jars of *Reine Claude* or *myrtille* while admiring the garden, absorbing the intoxication of smells, the unbottled perfume of lavender, pine and sage. Others too fed morsels to intrepid birds, walked the hot summer Sunday roads of the Cap that lead to rocks, where now they could plunge, float, dream and burn in the sun, and then walked back and heard and tasted and dreamed and woke with the shrilling arpeggios of the sparrows and pointed out to each other exotic flowers.

You will cherish the memory and the memory will feed you its moments of the innocent time when all you wanted was a clear sky, the wicker chair, long meandering sun–filled walks … scratched by the briars, clawed by the branches, stung by the mosquitoes, chafed by the wind, bruised by the stones, cooled by the sea, astonished by the deep, and soaked by your sweat. After your shower you will look into the mirror and see the day has added its weight to your life until one day you will sink under it, another will sit in your chair and stare and feed the sparrows and open miniature jars of *Reine Claude*.

RASCALS

As usual there is the fluttering of people going in and out of this large institution – since these ancient Jewish delis are gathering places for the old Jewish world. Now I can see the odd old crapper shuffling along, reluctant to lift a foot even an inch off the floor, scraping his slow way as if he were sanding it – and I can hear the raspy sound long after he has passed me. I approach and see that there is a group queuing at the door – although it is only mid–afternoon – and judging by their advanced age you might believe that they were waiting for attention outside a hospital. I can observe a constant coming and going from doors situated on opposite sides of the single–storey building, the restaurant symbolising the human body since you enter at one end and exit by the other. Squeezing the metaphor even more – a cash desk is situated at the exit; therefore your vital monetary nutrition is extracted from you before you are evacuated. Near the mouth where I stand and wait are two lines, one for tables and one for the very large counter. Most people are opting for tables and booths where they can face each other and yack. The mouth is slowly swallowing the long tongue of the queue and eventually I am deposited in the huge stomach of the building. There are two huge rooms seemingly full of people happily munching away and steady babble fills the air.

At the head of the queue stands an elderly female MD who occasionally strides up and down like a sentinel as if her life had reached a point of no return and is thus condemned forever to parade the Isles of Deli. Her face seems to be at the apotheosis of magnificent decadence and reminds one of an aged crocodile, mouth open as if she were in the middle of some abstract conundrum or pained by a decision of overwhelming magnitude when actually all she is trying to do is breathe. Arthritis has curved her spine and placed an envious mountain on her back; her hips seem to be rusted as she strides with a stiff but purposeful gait, yet on the brink of disintegrating into dust like a mummy exposed to air for the first time in 3,000 years. This Jewish mummy by the effect of an iron will forces those molecules to grip each other. Her fingers are bejewelled believing this adds adamantine solidity and her earrings are long, gross and could be called Jewish–Gothic. Her lips are a crude slash of red and her glasses are as huge as they can be with those handles that look as if they are worn upside–down. There is a marvellous corruption of all human culture in this woman and one feels that all the influences of the Middle East, Europe and even America have flowed together to spawn her. She sadly looks like a fascinating junk room of Western civilisation and yet what defines her character is an intense Jewishness, the full flowering of the ghetto. She is one of the many whom centuries of confined environments have interbred; a slender, attenuated and hawkish creature whose nerve centres are spun out to receive the finest vibrations. Her features seem to be made with the thinnest paste and yet her dark eyes glow with an indomitable will to live. Ageing has not given her the dignity of some equivalent gentile lady who, with watery blue eyes and pinkened cheeks, can waddle to the church bazaar in her grandmotherly way. No, this is Dracula, dragon, Babylonia and anxiety taken to stress levels that would kill most people. She wears a satin trouser suit and her stage is the grease–sticky floor of Rascals where corned beef is sliced by the ton each year and the munching millions return to the solace of love food.

I have never in my life seen so many old people in one restaurant or one place. It is a sanctuary for the elders but more than that – it is a graveyard, the grey ones' meeting place, almost a wake for their youth. I think the reason the old Miami Jews don't seem to age gracefully is that they refuse to! They have a compulsive need to beautify themselves beyond the grave; hair tinted a purply lavender or a straw–stiff blonde, the same colour I recall my poor mother dyeing her hair for so many years until it resembled tufts of grass but one day she gave up the habit and it turned a dignified silver. Is it the Eastern, Polish or Russian influence that impels Jewish women to try and retain the vestiges of youth even within the ravages of age, or did the squalid life in the teeming East Ends of cities demand that you be attractive? Was the fear of being left unwanted, of such unthinkable dread that the rouge, lipstick and dye became the allies of the housewife? The intensity of ghetto life drove young women to compete with their sisters with feverish desperation and even in the ghetto of Rascals, the aged seem bent over and crippled, crushed beneath the weight of illness and woe. It is still the East Side of New York and the East End of London with a hairdresser on every corner. If you cannot alter your face or environment at least you can make a masterpiece of your hair.

Since I am alone I am seated by the great Jewish crow and find myself in the centre of the oval–shaped counter. On my right is a strong–looking but weathered Jewish man with dyed hair sitting with his wife – he looks Russian – and on my left are two men in their seventies who still have a vitality beyond their years; a vitality of the pill, perhaps, since their faces are already turning a parchmenty white. I order a corned beef sandwich, my rare indulgence and ordered only in delis. The man on my right finds his corned beef sandwich rather large and, as I crunch on the free bowl of pickles, I sneak a look and observe him scoop out excess slabs of the meat, using his finger and thumb, and plonk it on his wife's plate – whom he has obviously typecast as a human garbage disposal unit. Suddenly the meat looks obscene, the crude gesture defiling what looked respectable in the sandwich now looks raped with slovenly indifference. However, since she has been a garbage bin all her life, the woman accepts the offering and immediately scoops it into her mouth without attempting to dignify it between two slices of rye. I carry on crunching from the mound of pickles in the aluminium bowl.

The queue for the tables is still long and from my barstool I can examine all the elders who are all grateful that another day has been blessed unto them and they can eat *kosher* deli. Although there are one or two younger ones, and some middle–aged, the rest are elderly – but an intense elderly that only a Jew pickled in angst, anguish, despair, *gavalt* and dread can have. An I–have–heard–and–seen–it–all face of no surprises – so here is undiluted age, heavy age, age that has grown up in the shade, in dusty cities, the cholesterol overkill of chicken soup and meatballs, on work and more work, compulsive and debilitating work and on the guilt that is the legacy of a hounded soul. Guilt for pleasure when the world is full of hells. Guilt for living and guilt for sex, guilt for not making your children *menschen*. But the guilt is too strong to take and must be diluted with the humour of death and the humour of the gallows; 'I want to be buried under the pavement of Bloomingdales so that I know my wife will visit my grave three times a week!'

The sandwich arrives and is excellent and the staff

are all clean–looking, alert, middle–aged and with a splattering of blacks. Traditionally blacks are seen in a way to be like Jews – emotional, overcooked Jews perhaps, big bosomy Jews and comfortable to be with, hence their love of *kosher* deli. The man on my right, the meat picker, lets out an involuntary belch, not huge but he quickly says, 'Excuse me.' I cannot help but visualise the home; the squashed sofa where for years he sits in the afternoon watching basketball, emitting an occasional belch which sends his wife scurrying to the cupboard to get a pill for his ulcers. A terrible familiarity reigns whereby all is permissible when the preservation of dignity is no longer an obligation – since for whom does one have to be dignified? The inhibiting filters that held up the grunge have long since rusted and what is left is unspeakable and sadly incontinent. Because there is no pain to which the Jew has not been exposed by knowledge, by empathy, by sympathy, by identification, and no pain has been too great, no humiliation too unspeakable, so the horror might leave one with an occasional indifference to niceties. Or, if not that, to the requisite codes of conduct that are deemed to be acceptable in polite society. So, 'Eat darling. Enjoy!'

BREAKFAST AT ITALA'S

Breakfast was always the best time and I can distinctly recall the breakfast my mother used to cook up for me when, as a rather finickity toddler, I was terribly partial to my daily fried tomatoes on toast. It was a very piquant taste as I remember and I gulped it down with cups of milky tea and this satisfied me then and ever since. When I left home to fend for myself, I would go round the corner to Itala's little café which sat on the edge of Colebrooke Row in Islington, North London. She greeted me with a large smile that seemed to dissect her face and her son Tony would take my order, invariably it would be an egg on toast with a sausage on the side. She would buzz around her domain chatting and smiling at the customers who were all drawn to the amiable woman and her son until we all became part of her surrogate family.

She would ask after Annie, and then when Annie

was no longer with me she was introduced to Shelley, and when Shelley and I were no longer together she met Helen and this went on. For a short time and she would always ask with a soft and suggestive smile how Shelley was because she liked Shelley and another day, with equal warmth, she would enquire after Annie, as if this was her favourite daughter and then another day it would be Helen. With a slightly different tone for each, it was as if she gauged my feelings and found the apposite note to make the enquiry.

On a sunny day she would put a solitary table outside and then we could pretend to be in the South of France. Sometimes it was scrambled eggs and tomatoes and then there was a time when she grilled cheese on toast for me – and that was delicious and, for a while, my preferred breakfast dish. If it wasn't too busy, I would sit at the corner table and write and occasionally exchange a few words with Tony. He was one of those people who knew someone for whatever you needed – electrician, karate teacher, builder, carpenter and so on – and would sit with me for a while, but never too long since he was sensitive to your needs and knew when the air was getting tight around us. Then the odd local would come in, like the writer who lived round the corner and wrote a screenplay called *Throb* and continuously and enthusiastically asked me to read *Diary of a Hero* by Lermontov. There were sunny days and I'd get up, feed the cat and really look forward to my breakfast in Itala's. I knew it would be tasty until one day she got rid of the grill for some unknown reason and I could no longer have my melted cheese on toast, heightened sometimes by a slice of lean ham on it. I was most disappointed.

In a lull, Itala would speak of vast changes she hoped to make to create the perfect environment for this charming little front room and every few years her fantasies would be fulfilled and she'd look at you eagerly for approval; once an effect of stained glass windows, another time a complete change of furniture. I first discovered this café when rehearsing *Macbeth* in a church on Devonia Road and went in there for a crate load of take–away teas. She had just moved in and the tables were sewing–machine bases but these were soon got rid of. Years later she bought a small dog which still barks ferociously for its size and seems to have a mean temper.

When I moved back to the regenerated East End, I visited her less and less but on occasion, I'd go and say hello to Tony and ask if he was getting married to that girl he'd courted for over 10 years. He has now, and made the final move away from mum, I imagine. I recall all the customers who became part of her family, the showroom designers from next door who became friends just because we met in Itala's. One of them looked me up when I was directing *Agamemnon* in Israel and he was charming, funny and very gay – sadly the last I heard of him was that he was dead. I must go back there, since I visited her café for over 15 years! Unbelievable. I had more breakfasts with her than with my own mother but, in a way, she was a kind of universal mother and when in one of my unhappy, romantic states she would accommodate her thoughts to suit my mood and reflect. 'That woman wasn't for you,' and 'The other one was much nicer.' She saw and sees everything and the last woman I brought in also said hello – but she didn't like to go out for breakfast as much as I did.

I'd go out, buy *The Guardian* and enjoy reading it from cover to cover and lingering over breakfast if I wasn't working and I had nothing else to do. I desperately wanted to be a Shakespearean actor and did audition after audition for the Halls and Nunns and whoever else stood in for them but got nowhere. Now I am a director and direct my own plays including Shakespeare, and I am still naive enough to ask for a space to bring my own productions but still curiously enough still get nowhere and so never learn. Build your own church. But it was in Islington that I started to be independent in the church hall where we were rehearsed each evening from 5pm until 10. I would sit with my assistant Chris Munke, a highly intelligent young American, and we would drink Itala's teas and eat her toast and the conductivity of the atmosphere led us always to some good solutions. I was sorry to lose Chris, who eventually drifted into the outer regions, and the last I heard of him he was teaching. But Itala was always there for me and for us, for words of cheer and words of comfort, for concern and curiosity. Yes, I want to go back there now, even as I write this, and I know she will say, 'And how is that woman who went to America and used to sing?' They often talked of opening in the evening as a bistro; this was a small fantasy which fuelled many a debate and one day I do believe they tried it, but it did not work out so well since Itala's was really an upmarket Italian greasy spoon café, which is not to diminish it, since that kind of working–class to middle–class food was the best you could get.

Recently I thought I would pop in on one of my occasional sojourns to Camden Passage Antiques Market and it was no longer there. Another bistro has opened in its place. It was a strange feeling as if part of my life had been erased, but my memories of Itala's café will probably remain with me forever.

ALFREDO'S

If I didn't go to Itala's, feeling a little like a traitor I would sneak into Alfredo's round the corner on the Essex Road; a symphony of Formica, hot, glistening and steaming machines for your tea – few drank wretched coffee in those days.

The yellow–topped tables were laid out military fashion, and I would take my usual seat and stare out of the window, equipped with my *Guardian* newspaper, full of hunger and expectation since I was up with the workers of the world and, in some strange way, could try to imagine that I too had a purpose in life, at least for the first hour. I'd watch the packed buses through the steamed–up windows, number 38 or 171, trundling along like old cart horses to the West End and order my usual, which in those days was a toasted liver and tomato sandwich. Oh the joy, the malty crunchy taste, slivers of liver welded to hot tomatoes, with a mug of tea served by the overworked blonde wife of Alfredo's son who, with blustery face and sweaty brow, took orders and shouted them back to the kitchen area situated just behind me. That was a good way to start the morning, and it was a ritual that saw me mostly alone in those far off days, which wasn't that pleasant, and for the life of me I can't recall why I was alone so much, and didn't have the night's companion with me. Perhaps when I did have a companion we would have breakfast in the warm kitchen, with the gasfire spluttering away, and for Alfredo's working–class men, a female was definitely out of place until Islington got so trendy that it became the in place for ladies, especially *Guardian*–reading ones, to flash their working–class sensibilities. So I would head up the road, and dive, especially on those cold wintry mornings, into the warm womb of the café.

Alfredo, the guv, would invariably be there, pottering behind the counter since he was getting on a bit, but found the razzmatazz of the café irresistible. He would buttonhole me with some theory, philosophy or a profound piece of economic wisdom, sometimes around the subject of the 'tanned races'. So I would sit there enjoying mightily my usual toasted liver and tomatoes, and sometimes introduce the odd friend to the exquisite delights, but when the breakfast was over I did not have the second stage to go to. In other words, I had no work, and my particular road went only so far, and so, invariably, I would turn back down St Peter Street as bleak a vision as you could possibly imagine

Alfredo's

to one out of work, and head into Devonia Road, N1, another even bleaker vision!

It's a hard life when you're relying on the taste and sensibilities of others to employ you, and I soon learned that the only way to get out of this vicious circle of work, wait, hope, depression, work, wait and so on, was to do the bloody thing yourself. I would implore all young actors to find even a couple of mates and put on their own work, most importantly to work for nothing and pool their resources, that will give them real strength. But at that time I had no actors to work with, and the kind of courage I needed to get going had not quite filled my tank. But writing was at least some kind of panacea, and I found myself writing a play which came to be known as *East* because it was set in the East, not necessarily in the East End of London, but in the East which is first smacked by the sun in the morning and where, for some particular reason, the slums are. So I decided to write whatever came into my head regarding the deepest pleasures of the British working–class kid.

Once I got into the theme so to speak, it began to flow. My method was to choose the highlights of a young man's life, and a young woman's, and naturally this would seem to centre on those activities which most fuelled testosterone explosion. So in drawing on some of my own experience, which was as different as can be imagined from a writer in England writing for the theatre, it was as if this particular age of youth never even existed, or was a dead zone as far as the establishment was concerned. And so they waited until the fires had been banked and were smouldering before the characters were thought worthy of depicting. My selection was perhaps pretty obvious, being the adrenalin–drawing activities, the battleground where young men would go to some private place and battle it out. On the few occasions it had been my lot when, with jelly–like knees, I wandered round the back of a cinema for the traditional toe–to–toe.

So, when returning from Alfredo's I would get out my notebook and make my jottings, but it never satisfied me that much since writing seemed like a pass–time to fit in when sitting in a café, but acting, learning lines, getting out before an audience while shitting yourself, this seemed like real work. So I decided that when I went to Alf's for breakfast, I would take my notebook, and then it was not idling my time away at home, but working, and it seemed much easier to write in these circumstances, and the play was finished. But I did not have the faintest idea of how to stage it, and so I let it simmer in a drawer for a while until one day, sitting in Alfredo's with my faithful and loyal colleague Barry Philips, the idea came to us just to get on with it. We each read one of the two main parts and no actors could really have been more suited for the roles; I don't know why on earth we had waited so damned long. We recruited Barry Stanton, a vast, exuberant actor with a great RSC pedigree, who was as if to the manner born, and virtually took us by the scruff and got on with the thing when I was getting too high–faluting about it. Never shall I forget, or cease to be so grateful to the gargantuan and generous spirit of Mr Stanton. Robert Longden played mum according to my deeply held beliefs that East End mums turn into men! The beautiful Australian Anna Nigh was perfect as Sylv, and chastised me nightly if I showed any sign of being less than fearless. And so, with this intrepid team we opened at the Edinburgh Festival in 1975 and never really looked back. Les, one of the two main characters, was my *alter ego*, since my ma had named me Leslie, a first name which I thought rather limp. Fortuitously she had had the foresight to give me a middle name of Steven – so I was grateful for that and ripped out the first and took the second. Mike was the bolder and wilder character that I really wished to be, with motorbike and motor–mouth, and so I played Mike. Les has a speech in which he describes a bus journey, the number 38 to be exact, which used to go past Alfredo's Café and which, for many years, was my ferry from the West End to the North. As he describes the journey he does not fail to mention Alfredo's – 'passed Alfredo's café, which makes great toasted liver sandwiches' … Oh yes...

After the play opened I actually bought a second–hand trial bike and then gradually I exchanged each bike for larger and larger machines until I became, to an extent, a pale facsimile of the character Mike that I played.

So Alfredo's seems not only a way of analysing your life but also a way of reconstructing it! But then you have to play the character until gradually it permeates into your being. The play was published and Alfredo, I believe, was also proud to have his greasy spoon café immortalised in my humble work and it soon became visited by any number of geeks and others who said they read or heard about the café from my play! At least that's what Alfredo said. The café, like many aspects of Islington, has been sold and it's now a slightly more upmarket greasy spoon but the tables are the same and the food is still good.

JUNIOR'S

Junior's in Brooklyn used to be a pretty cool place to go, but of late it seems to have lost its shazam. Nevertheless, it's still a must place to visit when you're in New York. There's always something going on, something to catch the eye of a deli–wanderer, and it's a must on Sunday, after a stroll along Coney Island from Brighton Beach. Stop off in Brooklyn and head to Junior's, where you will catch the grand procession of Afro–Americans, honed and dolled up for Sunday church. An air of high expectancy hovers over the tables with the plump black ladies dressed up to the hilt, their men in polka dot bowties and the kids white sox and polished shoes. Since a Jewish deli also doubles as black soul too, and Jews and blacks forget their bitter differences and the poisonous words of black leader Farrakhan and realise that we share pretty similar taste buds. Well, Jews and blacks have the same bird in common, and while the

My Life in Food

Jews swim across a veritable red sea of chicken soup each year, their black cousins devour an India of chicken, rice and sweetcorn amongst other delicacies including Jewish deli.

So, once again, the humble bird features prominently at Junior's, and half the customers are now black, where once they were Polish, Russian or Rumanian. There is a déclassé ease in the deli, a simple and pleasant familiarity, the natural acceptance of Junior's as their place ... It's comfortable, easy, and normal, and lacks the starch whiteness of Protestant America, and since both races have born the brunt of Christian antagonism, there is in spite of the black's accusation of Jew–shark landlords, a kindred spirit.

So the Jew is, in some senses, the buffer between black and white rage, and is often accused of shylocking the blacks. There are occasional explosions, as when a Jewish funeral car, of all things, knocked down and killed a young black boy. All hell broke loose, and there were reprisals, but here now at Junior's we are in neutral territory, the *schwartzers* and *hymies* are united at the temple of the joyous feast; an over–sized smiling sandwich, stuffed *knish*, overfilled bagels, chicken soup with *kreplach* – and is this soul food for it is the food of joy and taste and relish and sensuality?

It is also philosophical food, for it is the food of abundance, joy–filled, open mouthed, big–teethed crunches and fat sandwiches, here we open wide our jaws, grin and chatter like monkeys and remind ourselves of the meanness of our own damp lands.

Here we laugh and recall our youth.

So when I heard that my production of *Salomé* had been booked to play at the Brooklyn Academy, the satisfaction I had was increased by the knowledge of its proximity to Junior's. My slow–motion production of Oscar Wilde's *Salomé* was cheered each night and we were proud, ecstatic, over the moon and delirious. We had just come from the Goodman Theatre in Chicago and I was taking my own company to New York for the first time; 1995. And yet each day when I came to the theatre it was too late to stop off and I couldn't really eat before the show anyway. It had been a rain–swelled week and nothing is really more depressing than New York in the rain and trying to hail a cab as cars squish past you, sending a fine spray of dirty water from the rots and potholes in the street.

So we'd do the show, take our bows to intense appreciation and then head back to our respective hotels. Saturday came, the last day, and my head was buzzing with what to do after the show. So I had booked a long table in Captain America and went round asking who would like to come, a ritual that I hate intensely, but at the same time I was determined to make our last night in New York memorable. Our administrator tried to talk me out of it since she couldn't really be bothered about such things, but for me the absence of a last night celebration would be nothing less than a crime. But it was a matinee day and in between afternoon and evening shows we would certainly visit Junior's for the last time.

My Life in Food

And so we did, with great anticipation and enthusiasm since I wished to show my English guys the wonders of America. As each actor was coming in his own time, I headed down the street with just one of them, while the others were washing their white make-up off. We found a nice booth right near the window and I ordered a corned beef sandwich for the hell of it, with trimming and side dishes of pickles and coleslaw. I was pleased to show them this landmark, this piece of iconography, the holy piece of Brooklyn where once a tree grew! Yes, the sandwich arrived and was predictably large, although not in the same gargantuan league as the Carnegie Deli in Manhattan, but still quite ample enough, and I offered my acting colleague a half of it. It rested on his pale moon of a plate with a wide pink smile.

Now the others were wandering in and joining us, and while waiting to order, I divided my half, forking the meat out delicately and placing it on some spare slices of rye that were in a basket. I noticed a famous American actress at the next booth, who had obviously seen the show but made no attempt to communicate which had me wondering whether she loved or loathed it, particularly me as Herod. But this is my paranoia peeking out. I was told she was Zoe Caldwell, of stirling reputation. Much American theatre lives and breathes with Mike Nichols, Zoe Caldwell, The Lincoln Centre and Chekhov revivals and so maybe I am beyond the pale.

Some other actors now dribbled in and we all sat

round while I made more and more sub–divisions of the original sandwich since there was so much of it. The English, accustomed as we were to the miserable tight–fisted English sandwich, were able to make a feast from these slabs of corned beef, while the crunchy pickled cucumber made a good companion. Then the coffee flowed, and soon the sky grew dark; meanwhile the theatre was refilling since we had had a sell–out show. We paid up, our bellies tight against our belts, and walked down Main Street Brooklyn, staring in awe at the wide variety of heavy–duty tracksuits made in ginormous sizes. The sandwich had really done us in and, being British, we had even thought of asking for a doggy bag to save the scraps for an interval nibble. There even seemed to be more at the end than in the beginning but we had to shrug this off as an optical illusion! Then, of course, it occurred to me that when Jesus fed his disciples, the loaves and the fishes were divided amongst his large audience and they too needed sacks to clear the debris. The answer was patently simple, and probably lay in the fact that when you are in a state of bliss, everything becomes enlarged, expanded, intensified, exaggerated, hyperbolised, and so too our simple corned beef sandwich. For even a single mouthful tasted like heaven; we were in the centre of the world, the giant megalopolis of New York, devouring history while playing Wilde's masterwork, his least known but, by him, best–loved play. We liberated Wilde from the bondage of the handbag play and *Salomé* was a feast. *Salomé* in Brooklyn. How very apt.

CHRISTMAS DINNER

So it comes around again and, again, there is the decision to make … here or fly off to the sun. So we stay and let's make the best of it. Clara, being born in Germany, still carries the memory of yuletide family gatherings, lit candles, masses of relatives and neighbourly visits, while I carried quite a different image. Mine was more an insufferable time of wait till it was over, deserted streets and ma and pa watching TV. When, as a child, I made some small effort to get excited and put up a stocking for Santa, I might get a small jigsaw puzzle and the rest was silence. Eventually it became a time of unmitigated gloom. But then it was different as for a few years we took off into the warm sweet sunshine of Madeira or the Caribbean and so escaped. This time we were going to do the whole damned thing, buy a turkey with all the trimmings and make our Christmas on Christmas Eve.

Christmas Dinner

But one should have some friends over to make it appear at least a little jolly but who to ask who wasn't scuttling off to their indifferent families which, at least, provided some cover for their loneliness – just in case there was no-one around to ask or to be asked by. Eventually I asked a very charming and recent acquaintance and his lovely lady and as he had a matinee that day it was quite convenient for him to cover over after the show. Perfect – and I felt a kindred spirit with this actor as did Clara.

Naturally, we scuttled off to Borough Market, which is an absolutely splendid piece of Victoriana on the south side of the river and not too far from the Globe old and new. The place is a sensation and only lacks the crowd bursting into song to resemble one of our British home-grown cosy musicals. The food tumbles out from all over and everything is of the best and highest quality. You're tempted as you stroll through at the vast tumbling cascades of veg to buy, as a multitude of vendors offer you a venison or buffalo burger, cappuccino or scallops, fishcakes or bagels. It's dense, vibrant, and noisy although a touch yuppie so it's a street market that feels working class but only in style and appearance. We bought a large, plump-looking turkey, seven kilos, at the phenomenal price of fifty quid. Then we gathered up carrots, herbs, sweet potatoes, turnips, *tommies*, cranberries, dates, figs, sage and onions for the stuffing and then went to an upstairs café for a simply delightful coffee and an appetizer of fried fish. We were on the first floor and could witness the stream of humanity pouring through the avenues of costermongers.

So far so good and we even found a place to park without some lousy traffic warden slapping a ticket on us within a minute of our getting there. Oh, we were in fine fettle and there's always something about a market that pulls you back into the warmth and swing of humanity, lest you become too cabined and confined in your cosy flat, supplied with Sky TV as a synthetic substitute for the rich earthly stench of humanity. How we need that and so, all my life, I have wandered through the markets of the world and after an immersion or a baptism I start to feel vaguely human again. The best markets in the world are probably in London although nothing can really beat the souk in Marakesh, a world on its own, and the flea market in Paris on the weekend is a pretty amazing event. I even worked off a market stall in London's Whitechapel as I mentioned in my memories of Joe Lyons. Getting home there is a feeling of being a touch depleted as if the injection of those rivers of flesh and blood has been too swiftly withdrawn.

Christmas Eve and my friend called and said he didn't have a matinee after all and therefore didn't need to come to London and, perhaps, we could make it for the following week … 'Sure, of course,' I easily responded as if there were just hundreds of merry fellows I could call on at the last minute to share our seven kilo turkey. 'Yes, we'll do it next week, no problem.' But, in fact, disappointment swiftly gave way to relief – we would just entertain each other, which we always do – no worry about entertaining, being a charming host, waiting for them to go – no – now we were off the hook. Free, that's OK but I felt more for Clara since I wished it to be a simple, friendly, warm Christmas ritual with smashing people, or even pleasant people, but the two of us is better than having to ring round to find some bums on seats.

When you have been conditioned from childhood on the misery of Christmas you somehow don't put the nuts and bolts in the right place. So I told Clara and she looked a tad glum but, typically, didn't show it and I said I'd call some mates. However, I decided to call my new friend back and say, 'Hey, couldn't you really make it since we may not be here next week and we don't want to have to eat this huge bird alone,' and all said with self–deprecatory winks and nudges and then he went on a bit about the train service on Christmas Eve and was making a really robust effort to charmingly decline as I was equally charmingly persuasive. Eventually he said that he would and would love to and I put the 'phone down and felt the clock had started ticking again. God, I was chuffed since it was all coming together. While most normal people would think nothing of a light piece of socializing, and how simple this is compared to putting on a play and getting a show together and acting, I have never really thought of myself as normal and so what is normal is reversed and the simple is intense, if not traumatic, and the traumatic is quite normal or at least more normal.

My Life in Food

To this mix, I added my pleasant part–time assistant as she had nowhere to go and then we were set–up.

On the morning of Christmas Eve, Clara got on with the zeal of a professional chef and in went the turkey, which we gazed on and thanked since she always does this, and we looked up the usual info from the cooking manual which was to give it 20 minutes per pound and so four hours would do it and we wrapped it in tin like a knight going into the fray. Gradually we added the usual ingredients and Clara, who is a vegetarian, nevertheless forswore her horror of touching the beast and readily and eagerly stuffed the stuffing up its posterior, the contents of which I had helped to adulterate somewhat. Everything went into that stuffing, sautéed shallots and celery, prunes, chestnuts and apricots, roasted pine kernels and cloves sprinkled with cinnamon with a dash of white wine and thyme and parsley. Clara rubbed groundnut oil onto its body, and nutmeg too, and we let it cook slowly for this was a prince of birds and at that price it was not to disappoint us. Our guests were due at 4pm.

Clara had already put together potatoes dauphinoise, which I hadn't even noticed and appeared as if by magic, and a bright mosaic of chopped veg were lying in a pan ready to be baked in the oven. The magnum of champagne, received on my sixtieth, was chilling in the freezer. I gently prodded the beast with fork and it sweated out its juices that we put in a pot for the gravy – most important this binds all. I threw into the gravy whatever came to hand, some seasoning, a dash of flour, a large dollop of paprika, wine, salt and let it slowly thicken and it tasted of childhood.

Oh yes, we were busy, and, oh yes, we had joined the human race once again; were preparing, we were giving, we were being allowed to share ourselves, our lives, our food and our love. How badly we needed to do this. Yes, we were in the mix. And on this day we felt ourselves to be a tiny but vital part of the puzzle and yet who could not be aware of those alone on that day, those ill on that day, and those without wives, or women, or men or children who are alone that day, alone on that particular day, when everybody boasts and bloats and belches. And that ragged small tree in the front room and the exposure of what you are, what you have, who loves you and all exposed on this, the cruellest of seasons! For some anyway.

But for now we were in the mix, the stew, the grease, the veg, the wine, the pies, the salad, the port, the stuffing, the gravy and so, yes we were part of the ensemble. Yes! The past has gone, the poor and grim and heartless empty Christmases are a thing of the past and now all is to be fulfilled.

And so we were busy, Clara and I, and particularly Clara. She was in her childhood's past in her home with her mother and father and brother in their lovely house in the Germany countryside making a happy and busy Christmas Eve altogether. And so, in her, this careful tradition was passed on and how carefully she passed it on and with what detail and affection does she carry this little piece of Germany inside her.

My Life in Food

For a few moments she becomes the mother of her past and, while I unfortunately carry another image; an immigrant image. Even if we have been here for a century, an image of alienation and sadness – although this is eroding, paling, disappearing as her stronger image takes over and I gain a new one.

The smell of our dear bird is pervading the house and we open the windows as the cat runs up and down excitedly and in great anticipation. My nice assistant comes first and immediately there is a change in the currents of air in the room as a new life enters. I ring my friend's mobile and they are on the way. They overshot and were sucked into the long intestines that links Poplar with Canary Wharf and had to go round all over again. They'll be here soon! My mind is agog as certain decisions are buzzing around my head. Leave it, just leave all those things behind. I step into the street and see a neighbour whose car window has been smashed in by vandals talking to a policeman feeling wounded – but then they arrive! They come bearing gifts! So many gifts: chocolates, a beautiful etching and a bottle of wine. My assistant also came with a gift and I am much moved since it never occurred to me that we would receive as well as give. So they came in and all was well. They smiled and beamed and drank a toast of my birthday champagne which tasted quite phenomenal. And the actor was in his element being articulate, knowledgeable and a comic, he was singing for his supper and out of his mouth came a tapestry of stories, anecdotes and jokes. The vegs went in and before long, not too long, we were summoned to the table upon which Clara had laid a pristine white cloth.

I removed the divine creature, our beautiful free range bird knowing it had passed a pleasant and untroubled life until sacrificed for us. I took it out and it felt stout and solid and was perfectly done. I sliced it and laid the soft, warm, tender slices on a large plate, followed by the veg and the sauce.

And yes, it really tasted amazing! Utterly delicious and, for a while I forgot myself and became immersed in the food for never had I tasted anything quite so wonderful. The veg had been baked in the oven and retained the essence of their taste, and the wine embraced all and the talk rose and fell. I was enamoured of our feast with the tastes that seemed to explode in my mouth; the purple cabbage, the sweet potatoes, the exquisite stuffing. And so we feasted but feasted in a way that we would never normally feast. We feasted as if there was something special to celebrate, like a birth or a wedding. It was a special feast because we were, of course, celebrating a birth – a unique birth. The birth of hope and the birth of something that has a fleeting resemblance to love. And thank God another Christmas had passed.

LIFE ON THE HIGH SEAS

Being an actor frequently gives one an opportunity to get close to food since casual work as waiter, dishwasher or barman has a quick turnover and there are always jobs to fill in at a moment's notice. But even before such times I found work in the catering industry, generally unskilled as a waiter on board cruise ships. The work was sheer hell and I certainly wasn't used to such labour. I signed on at Tilbury to work on the Mediterranean cruises which is about the very worst work you can do, as you're on the go from morning till night.

I bought my ship's uniform and turned up for work on a liner call the Chusan, a great beast of a ship, full of the scallywags of the earth, down and outs, ex soldiers, conscientious objectors and all the flotsam and jetsam that gravitate towards the catering industry as waiters and short order cooks. My first group came in and I

Life on the High Seas

was responsible for two tables seating four at each. You would think that wasn't too much of a burden but, for some obscure reason, we weren't allowed to write down the orders but simply to remember them, as if that made it a bit posher. Try remembering eight different orders and the variety of petty requests although, to speak true, the meals were mostly a choice of two or three mains, and pretty awful at that. Since I was the last to finish on the first breakfast, I was put on the very first table next to the kitchen and I still managed to be the last table still eating when the rest of the dining room was deserted.

First off we were woken at 6am. Down to the dining room, mop and clean our area, set the tables, wolf down a sausage and toast and be ready as the hungry eager faces poured to their tables. As soon as you're finished, it's back to the cabin for a quick rest, a shower, a fag and then it's time to set up for lunch! Now that was more complex and to save time I'd bung a few plates of soup into my dumb waiter, that cupboard at the end of your station where you keep plates and silver, thinking that if I got the soup out double quick I'd be amongst the first to get the entrees out. God I was hopeless but the passengers seemed to have a little pity for me, thank God, and tolerated with wry amusement my bitter struggles.

Each meal time was divided into two sessions so no sooner had the first lot finished then the next lot were in, while the first lot took coffee in the lounge. It was hell to get the first lot finished while the second lot were champing at their teeth to get their nosh.

Then your first break, just flopping out on the deck in the staff area, shattered, exhausted and feeling hopeless. The others were tougher. They had been doing it, some of them for years, and were fast and fit and had time to be funny and entertain the eaters, working for their big end of the trip tip. They looked wiry, clever, smart duckers and divers, while I just sweated and clutched up my stomach that was always in pain with the bloody duodenal ulcers that were just emerging.

We're going from port to port, and if we were lucky there was no more work until the evening but some of the buggers would come back in little ferries just for their tea time and so you'd have to scuttle back. Then they could sit anywhere to be served tea, so you didn't have to face your disgruntled customers more than was necessary.

We arrived one morning in Barcelona and never had I seen anything more beautiful than that early golden glow over the harbour. I couldn't wait to get out there in the street since we all had the morning off after breakfast as everybody was going ashore, and this was what after all they had paid for. So after breakfast I put on my civvies and, strolling up the great Rambla, I felt somewhat human again.

Abroad was exciting, mysterious, exotic and the Rambla was full of sun, heat, food, cafés, bars, people and before I knew where I was I found myself gazing at this delicious fully–shaped woman with a body hugging

Life on the High Seas

dress. I was just staring at her and, lo and behold, she stared back at me with fearless abandon and beckoned me to go with her. I needed little prompting as she was so lusciously gorgeous and in no time I found myself in her quite pleasant flat, thoroughly enjoying some delightful Spanish tapas. These were so wonderfully moreish that within seconds I found myself wanting seconds … I was a young vigorous man and obviously had quite an appetite which even she remarked on with some little admiration. I was after all just 19. After such an unusual and tasty meal I was in a very relaxed mood, when I went back to that awful ship which by now felt like hell.

Some nights when we had finished work we were allowed out on the town, we used to stare at this beautiful sight of the liner lit up, looking proud and elegant, almost dream-like. We'd all agree with the idea that such a beautiful image could in fact contain an inferno within.

However, after a few more days had passed, I found myself not feeling on top of the world, especially after that tapas in Barcelona. It must have been slightly contaminated as I was possessed by a goddamn awful itching. Of course, I could have caught this on the boat, with our confined quarters and just one loo! I was glad to get home and swiftly got well again. It was an adventure for sure but I don't think I would fancy another trip, except as a tourist.

SIMPSON'S–IN–THE–STRAND

Simpson's–in–the–Strand is a posh place, to whose embalmed and traditional British atmosphere I had been introduced by a catering agency in Charing Cross Road. I loved these agencies since you never knew where you would go next, into what hallowed atmosphere your low, scummy self would be needed! To be employed and paid … ahh yes. One day I was told that they required some part–time commis waiters there, and had I a decent dress suit etc, to which I replied of course, and made my way there. A commis waiter is basically the bottom of the scale of the pecking order, just above cleaners and dish washers, since you do have to make an appearance clearing up dishes and delivering them, setting up the cutlery, laying the tables and bringing the deserts, but never taking orders. I turned up as requested and changed immediately into my dinner jacket, white shirt and black bow, but alas I did not have suitable black shoes, so I donned a smart pair of brown ones, and anyway who would notice in the hustle and bustle as long as the rest was OK. So after changing I got into line in the kitchen to collect the orders, mainly the veg and salads since the meat was elegantly cut at the tables by the top waiters, with a sharp carving knife and plonked onto the customer's plate.

This was the grand Simpson's tradition … the great silver trolley is wheeled to the table, the casket containing the meat is opened, the large knife selected and the meat is sliced off in thick pink slabs. So I went about my business for an hour or two, when the head waiter, a man who took the position of actor–manager of the room and in whose kingdom we are but humble serfs, beckoned me over and gave me a withering glance from his fishy cold blue eyes and then bent his head slightly towards the floor, pointing at the same time with his finger at something you would have thought must be some unspeakable horror but in fact he was merely pointing at my brown shoes! He stared down at my shoes and said 'You're wearing brown shoes, that's not acceptable … you knew the dress code', and I was summarily dismissed. There's a certain tradition in such hallowed institutions such as Simpson's that you dare not breach. One of them being that you do not, ever, under any circumstances don a pair of brown shoes. Black, black and always black. Spick and polished. I was, of course, well aware of that particular commandment, but sadly the only decent pair of shoes in my possession

My Life in Food

at that time were a smart pair of brown shoes with elasticated sides, so beloved of sporting types and BBC producers, and in the hustle and bustle I thought they would not be noticed.

I do believe I was informed on by an irate customer, who must have felt that the empire was falling apart by my unintentional assault on tradition … So the head waiter repeated 'I shall have to let you go.' I felt no anger since he was of course, absolutely right. It is verily these men, who are the watchdogs of the Empire and hold it together. Simpson's–in–the–Strand is still there and hopefully will be there for years to come. In fact, I'd love to go back there but not as a waiter but as a fawned–over customer. I've always had this need to return to the scene of the crime.

EXTRACTS

A list of original sources of extracted and modified stories.

Wolfie's
Extracted in its entirety from *Shopping in the Santa Monica Mall*, chapter 17, pages 122 – 127.

Churrascaria
Extracted in its entirety from *A Prisoner in Rio*, pages 68 – 71, with a short introduction added for this book.

Homage to Grande–Hotel
Adapted extract from *Shopping in the Santa Monica Mall*, chapter 20, pages 138 – 142.

Rascals
Extracted in its entirety from *Shopping in the Santa Monica Mall,* chapter 7, pages 39 – 43.

Breakfast at Itala's
Adapted extract from *Shopping in the Santa Monica Mall,* chapter 21, pages 143 – 146.